BURNOUT TO BRILLIANCE

Burnout to Brilliance could save your life. Author Jayne Morris offers the rationale, the reasoning and the tools to enhance your life. It's informative, easy to read and packed with ideas from someone who's been there, done it and proudly wears the T-Shirt.

Michael Heppell, number-one speaker and success coach

When we're overwhelmed by the busy-ness of everyday life, it's easy to feel disconnected from our innate happiness, brilliance, and love. The result: depletion or burn out. If you want a life that feels vital, alive, and aligned with your dreams, meet Jayne Morris. In *Burnout to Brilliance*, she clearly shows the way.

Marci Shimoff, professional speaker and New York Times bestselling author, *Happy for No Reason, Love for No Reason*, and *Chicken Soup for the Woman's Soul*

Burnout is endemic in the NHS and other public services, and it is important that ways are found to reduce it. This book is a valuable contribution, filled with vital information and tactics for a stress free working life. A must read!

Dr. Clare Gerada, Immediate Past Chair, Royal College of General Practitioners

What a great book to deal with the "do it all" culture! Jayne lets us know that doing it all comes with a hefty price.

Michelle Gayle, actress, writer, and singer

In *Burnout to Brilliance*, Jayne Morris elegantly shares how change is possible, balance is attainable and your passion for life can be restored. In a voice that is resonate with hope and gentle encouragement, this book will help you rediscover your passion that leads you on to the path of your destiny.

Janet Bray Attwood, New York Times bestselling co-author of *The Passion Test: The Effortless Path to Discovering Your Life Purpose*

I believe the connection between mind and body is close, powerful, and offers a valuable tool in taking control of your life and ambitions. With a rare sense clarity and compassion, *Burnout to Brilliance* explores that connection through teachings and stories that illuminate, inspire and are genuinely accessible. Thank you, Jayne Morris, for sharing your voice and experience with the world.

Dr. David R. Hamilton, Ph.D., scientist, motivational speaker and author of *How Your Mind Can Heal Your Body* and *Is Your Life Mapped Out?*

Stop running for your life and start savouring your life with *Burnout to Brilliance*. Jayne Morris combines recent research with real life insights and effective tools for stepping back from the busyness of your routine to re-examine what's important and how to use your precious time on the things that really matter.

Sandy C. Newbigging, bestselling author of *Heal the Hidden Cause* and *Mind Calm*

Burnout to Brilliance is essential reading for all those feeling trapped in a life of busyness. Author Jayne Morris combines leading research, expert analysis and profoundly personal messages that clearly signpost the route to avoid burnout and will help you to navigate the way to your own innate brilliance. Jayne has lived these lessons and now shares her wisdom in an accessible, fun and engaging manner. I cannot recommend it highly enough.

Professor Damian Hughes, Professor of Organisational Behaviour and Change, Manchester Metropolitan University

If you find yourself never having enough time, going to bed and waking up with a to-do list that keeps getting longer, and sensing burnout is looming close, this book is written for you. Full of practical tools this book is for real people living real lives, this is an excellent handbook on how to avoid hitting that wall. A must read to survive the rat race!

Mary Daniels, co-director of Alternatives, the UK's leading event organisers for inspirational talks and workshops

Brilliance is not a result of busyness. In fact, it's quite the opposite. When we are able to slow down and come from the centre of our being, our achievements have a different quality to them. Our successes become fulfilling, sustainable and reflect a tangible grace and elegance that in turn inspires others. In *Burnout to Brilliance*, Jayne Morris shows us how this is possible.

Nick Williams, author of *The Work We Were Born To Do* and founder of the Born to Lead Community

Burnout to Brilliance deserves a spot on everyone's bedside table. Filled with useful strategies that address body, mind and spirit, it essential reading for anyone in breakdown mode. Jayne Morris beautifully maps the journey to brilliance for us, showing us that it's possible to change our life course and discover the place where long-lasting healing, balance and rest resides.

Karen Brody, critically acclaimed playwright and founder of BOLD Tranquility and BOLD Birth

Jayne's delightful book is written from the heart. With raw honesty, she shares her experiences her remarkable journey and personal story of recovery from burnout. As one who has experienced burnout on a number of occasions and attempted to push through, believing I only needed to work harder to reach my goals, *Burnout to Brilliance* rang many bells. Jayne encouraged me to rethink my game plan by showing a productive but softer way forward. I love this book!

Anne Jirsch, author of *The Future is Yours*

Jayne Morris's book is a godsend to anybody dealing with high-pressure situations, or experiencing being overwhelmed by any aspect of life. It provides a wide range of simple, practical and effective solutions for avoiding or getting over burnout. Because burnout and being overwhelmed are one of the major causes of chronic health, emotional crises, relationship, performance and addiction issues. As such, *Burnout to Brilliance* is essential reading.

Phil Parker, designer of the Lightning Process, author of *Get The Life You Love NOW*

A heartfelt, insightful and practical look at how and why we burnout and how to make the journey back towards optimal health, wellness and inspiration. I wholeheartedly recommend this book to clients and patients as well as keeping my own copy close to hand.

Dr Nerina Ramlakhan, author of *Tired But Wired* and Sleep and Energy Consultant to the Capio Nightingale Hospital

Burnout to Brilliance is a wise and compassionate book. Jayne Morris writes compellingly about how to listen to your body, mind and inner wisdom to heal your life. It's filled with new perspectives and effective techniques to guide you on a journey to a life of joy and peace.

Lynn A. Robinson, author of *Divine Intuition: Your Inner Guide to Purpose, Peace and Prosperity*

Jayne offers an urgently needed, hugely accessible and holistic solution to the problem of psychic and physical exhaustion confronting so many people today. We only have one life to enjoy

– don't let it pass you by in a haze of burnout! Learn to relish it and relax in to being alive, well and brilliant with Jayne's book.
Nick Bolton, founder of Animas Centre for Coaching

If you are on the road to burnout, stop and read this book. You will be back to brilliance in no time.
Sue O'Brien OBE, CEO Norman Broadbent

In a global culture obsessed with performance and results, Jayne Morris flips the script. *Burnout to Brilliance* offers a solution to the modern-day neurosis of busyness and gives us a healthy prescription for slowing down, having grace, and relishing in a life that we actually love.
Latham Thomas, founder of Mama Glow, author, *Mama Glow: A Hip Guide to Your Fabulous Abundant Pregnancy*

I don't anyone who would not benefit from reading this book. Jayne Morris writes with passion, knowledge and personal experience about how to escape burnout and find a more gentle and balanced way of living. It's a well-worn phrase, but this book really could change your life!
Kim Morgan, founder and Managing Director of Barefoot Coaching Ltd

Burnout to Brilliance is an absolute "must read". As a relationship expert with over two decades' experience working with people who are stressed out, I know firsthand that burnout inflicts pain upon your relationships with the people you love the most: your partner, your children and perhaps above all else – yourself! If you are feeling stressed out in any area of our life, run – do not walk – and invest in this book before it's too late and you burnout. You and your family are worth it!
Dr. Patty Ann Tublin, CEO and founder, Relationship Toolbox LLC

Jayne's brilliant and she's been burnt out. Jayne speaks with knowledge and from the heart. If you're feeling in any way burnt out, pick up this book now!

Nina Grunfeld, founder of Life Clubs

Burnout To Brilliance is a book you won't want to put down, you'll be so motived to change! Jayne Morris has a way of simplifying those things we make complicated. She artfully explores the science behind why we do what we do and spiritual journey that takes place when we are ready for change.

It's essential reading for anyone who is challenged with always being on the go.

Heather Chauvin BSW, parenting coach

Burnout to Brilliance

Strategies for Sustainable Success

Burnout to Brilliance

Strategies for Sustainable Success

Jayne Morris

CHANGE
MAKERS
BOOKS

Winchester, UK
Washington, USA

First published by Changemakers Books, 2015
Changemakers Books is an imprint of John Hunt Publishing Ltd., Laurel House, Station Approach,
Alresford, Hants, SO24 9JH, UK
office1@jhpbooks.net
www.johnhuntpublishing.com
www.changemakers-books.com

For distributor details and how to order please visit the 'Ordering' section on our website.

Text copyright: Jayne Morris 2014

ISBN: 978-1-78279-439-4

A CIP catalogue record for this book is available from the British Library.

Design: Stuart Davies

Printed in the USA by Edwards Brothers Malloy

We operate a distinctive and ethical publishing philosophy in all
areas of our business, from our global network of authors to
production and worldwide distribution.

CONTENTS

A Note from the Author

It is with incredible gratitude to my husband Dylan and to my family and friends for their patience, understanding and strength of support, which has enabled me to write and share this book with you.

Six years ago my body started to shut down due to years spent overworking and overcommitting myself in every area of my life. As a result I spent six months bedridden with labyrinthitis (extreme dizziness) and adrenal exhaustion.

Barely able to lift my head from my pillow, I had plenty of time to reflect on the internal beliefs and external circumstances that had led to my catastrophic burnout. It was the reality check that I needed.

I identified that many of the patterns and behaviours affecting my choices in life stemmed from a mantra I had learned in primary school: *Good, better, best. You will never rest. Until your good is better. And your better is best.*

Throughout primary school my ambition was to win as many gold stars as possible in order to impress my teachers. This continued into secondary school where I strived to win merits and awards. By university my underlying desire to please others and receive recognition for my efforts meant that it had become the norm for me to go above and beyond standard academic expectations.

The effects of this behaviour began to appear while I was at university. One day during my final year studies, I collapsed after a strenuous workout at the gym, suffering persistent headaches in the aftermath. I took a week off to recover. However, I soon resumed my demanding work and exercise patterns, continuing as if nothing had ever happened.

Upon graduation, I moved to Japan where I worked as a teacher and television presenter. It was a challenge to adjust to a radically different culture and climate, but my ambition to prove myself led me to continue with my desire to deliver excellence, routinely going above and beyond what was required of me. I had become addicted to overachievement. I set my own standards so high that people began to expect increasingly more from me. Work became an uphill struggle.

I continued to receive signs that I needed to slow down. One Monday morning after a weekend spent running a booth at an international festival, I recall literally heaving my body out of bed in order to drive to work. Only a few hundred metres from my apartment, a driver ran through a stop sign and ploughed into the side of my car, the impact causing severe whiplash. Yet, as soon as I had recovered, I resumed my previous fast pace.

A few months later while I was still struggling with injuries from the car accident, my body gave me another sign that I needed to prioritise rest. I woke one night with severe abdominal pain and was rushed to hospital. The doctors discovered an ovarian cyst the size of a grapefruit, which they operated on immediately for fear it could rupture at any given moment.

Recovery from the procedure took several weeks, but again, I subsequently returned to old habits of doing too much. When my three-year tenure in Japan came to an end, I flew back to the UK determined to pursue a career in television marketing, seeking out jobs with high-level entry requirements and correspondingly demanding schedules. Shortly after securing a position in brand management at the BBC, my unrelenting drive led to further physical and emotional exhaustion.

My body responded to the stress by sweating profusely while I was at work. I used to change my clothes three times each day, spending a small fortune on multiple identical outfits in order to keep my colleagues from noticing. I tried a variety of alternative therapies in an attempt to solve the problem ranging from acupuncture to a variety of unpalatable Chinese herbal remedies. Nothing seemed to help.

In 2007 I developed debilitating repetitive strain injury (RSI) in both of my wrists. As usual, I pushed through this constant pain, enduring it for several months. Eventually things got to the stage where my hands and wrists completely seized up.

Around the same time I had started a work place training course in life coaching, which I found fascinating. For the first time in my life I was taking the time to stop and reflect on my ambitions and what it was that I was *really* in pursuit of. I wanted to learn more about the psychology of coaching and enrolled in a masters level degree course in Personal and Business Coaching accredited by the University of Chester.

I handed in my notice at the BBC in order to pursue part-time coaching studies and returned to teaching, embarking on the Teach First programme for 'exceptional graduates' wanting to become part of a 'new generation of leaders both inside and outside of education'. Teach First pride themselves in their reputation for recruiting super self-starters from top universities, placing them in tough inner city schools where they are recognised for raising pupil aspirations and achievements through innovation and resourcefulness.

Without consciously realising what I was doing, I had jumped out of the frying pan and into the fire. The challenges of the programme were intense. I was already running on reserves and did not have sufficient fuel left in my engine to meet the demands either inside or outside of the classroom, let alone to maintain my part-time University studies in coaching. Existing on four hours of sleep a night caused my immune system to grow weaker and weaker. Eventually I caught a virus that rendered me bedridden and unable to function.

Burnout finally got the better of me.

I was confined to my bed, exhausted and often too dizzy to lift my head from my pillow. I felt stuck. Try as I might to get going again, I would take one step forward and two steps back. My hopes for a complete recovery began to fade.

After several months of debilitation I felt I needed some time away from the bed that had become my prison. I longed for a solution.

I began searching for retreat centers and stumbled upon a three-day course in Dorset designed to help people overcome fatigue. The programme was run by a Phil Parker *Lightning Process* practitioner named Lynn Atkins. I felt it might help me gain some inner direction because it incorporated elements of coaching and NLP, with which I was familiar. I registered for the course and anxiously awaited its arrival in June of 2008.

It proved to be just what I needed to help quiet my busy mind, go within and gain some clarity. For the first time in my life I paused my thoughts for long enough to pay attention to what my body wanted to communicate. I connected with what I can only describe as a 'deep inner wisdom'.

That decision to listen changed my life.

It was as if my body was talking to me and explaining that it had shut down because it could no longer trust my mind to look after it. In order to recover, my mind had to promise my body that it would continue to listen.

I decided to make that promise and make self-care a priority in my life.

By the end of the course, I felt ready to start my journey of self-discovery: a journey to find a different way to live my life. I instinctively knew I could not fix things with the same mindset that created the problem.

My perception of burnout had shifted from that of a curse to a blessing. Burnout became an opportunity to rediscover and reinvent myself.

I allowed myself to open to the possibility of profound personal change and deep inner healing. As a result, energy and enthusiasm quickly returned to my body.

I was no longer bed bound.

I felt inspired to resume my childhood passion for painting in order to continue accessing inner guidance. I found that this helped me to open my intuitive abilities and enabled me to more deeply explore my internal thought processes. I also drew upon powerful martial arts and meditation exercises that I had trained in for most of my life, but previously never taken outside of the dojo.

I resumed my postgraduate training in coaching alongside a masters level degree course in integrative art psychotherapy. These two programmes helped provide me with further tools and techniques that gave me clarity and purpose.

It felt as though all my previous life experiences had led me to a pivotal point from which I consciously chose the next step, rather than acting as if on autopilot. I remember thinking 'what if I could help other people connect with their power, passions and purpose so that they too could transform their lives from burnout to brilliance?'

While I was burning out I had not fully appreciated the detrimental effects that my previous patterns of overwork were having on every area of my life. Learning to live my life aligned with a sense of purpose and meaning changed everything.

By the beginning of 2009, I felt renewed, renergised, and reinspired. I was alive, aware and ready: my self-development business 'Power Up Coaching' was born.

Now, several years on, I'm thrilled and deeply grateful to wake up each day and be inspired by the work I do. I enjoy healthy, balanced and joyful relationships with friends and family. I am married to the man I love, to whom I am extremely grateful for being willing to stand by my side and believe in my potential to change. We enjoy spending so much more time together than ever before and have been blessed with a beautiful daughter. As I write this book we are excited to be expecting our second child.

Since starting my business I have felt humbled by the incredible people all over the world with whom I have been honoured to work. Time and again I have witnessed the miracle of personal transformation as a result of people from all walks of life addressing burnout, overcoming previous limitations and waking up to the gift of their lives as a journey for self-discovery, self-care and the fulfillment of passion and potential.

If you find yourself continuously feeling exhausted, overwhelmed and wondering whether there is another way, this book is for you. I have written it with the hope that it will help to renergise and reinspire you to live your life on purpose, connected to the essence of the incredible person you are truly here to be.

It is time to wake up and transform your life from burnout to brilliance!

Foreword

As someone who experiences stress nightmares when I'm run down and overly tired — and as one who firmly believes the architecture of how we live our lives is badly in need of repair and renovation—I'm always grateful to hear a reassuring voice from someone who not only shares the experience but embodies a path to renewal and recovery.

Jayne Morris lived the fast-paced and fast-tracked life that sadly has become the rule rather than the exception for many today. We wear our busyness with a false sense of pride, complaining to others about never having enough time, yet inwardly proclaiming our chaotic lives as an indicator of our self-worth and success. As a result, burnout, stress and depression have become worldwide epidemics.

"We are fast turning from a race of human 'beings' into human 'doings,'" Jayne wisely notes. Overwhelmed by the fast-paced and technologically demanding world in which we live, she says, we routinely run on reserves and force ourselves to accept that constantly feeling tired is all part and parcel of living a busy and "connected" life.

I couldn't agree with her more. We relentlessly push and press forward, eventually hitting the proverbial wall. The price we are paying for this way of thinking and living is far too high and unsustainable.

The founder of the *Huffington Post*, Arianna Huffington, relays her burnout story in her latest book, *Thrive*. She states that if you're lucky, you have a "final straw" moment before it's too late. Arianna's arrived in the spring of 2007, when she literally collapsed from exhaustion and lack of sleep onto the floor of her home office and found herself in a pool of blood from a head injury.

Ironically, Jayne's final straw came that same year, when she began to develop repetitive strain injury in her hands, wrists and

7

arms, perspiring so heavily that she had to change clothes three times each day. She subsequently developed post viral fatigue and labyrinthitis, and was bedridden for six months.

Arianna's personal "wake-up" call prompted a period of deep reflection, reevaluation, and ultimately, renewal as she reexamined her assumptions about work, the definition of success, personal priorities and what constitutes a meaningful and rewarding life.

Thankfully, Jayne's did as well. "Despite being exhausted physically and emotionally from burnout, as I slowly began to recover, I experienced something of an awakening," she writes. "In pushing myself to the limits, I suddenly realized that I could go no further unless I found a way to turn everything around. I connected with an internal longing to do so much more with my life, fuelled by the energy of creativity and inspiration."

Marie Asberg, professor that the Karolinska Institutet in Stockholm, describes burnout as an "exhaustion funnel" we slip down as we give up things we don't think are important. We all know the feeling. Overwork becomes a way of life, leaving us continuously feeling exhausted and depleted. Somewhere in the back of our minds, however, we realize that one by one, the moments in life that truly matter are passing us by.

Jayne began to re-examine her life and the passions that had fueled her work and interests over the years. As she reflected on key life experiences, previous challenges she had overcome, and the natural talents and the skills she had developed along the way, the pieces slowly began to fall into place. She ultimately was able to open to her true calling and purpose in life.

The editorial philosophy behind *HuffPost's* twenty-six Lifestyle sections is based on four pillars referred to as the Third Metric. We're all familiar with the primary metrics and measures of success in our society: money and power. However, to live the lives we truly want and deserve—and not just the lives we settle for—we need a Third Metric, a third measure of success that goes beyond the two metrics of money and power, and consists of four pillars: well-being, wisdom, wonder, and giving.

These four pillars allow us to connect with innate desire to engage with others and inhabit a new definition of a successful life. *HuffPost's* Lifestyle sections promote the ways that we can take care of ourselves and lead balanced, centered lives while making a positive difference in the world. We have a wide array of talented and gifted writes and authors who contribute to these sections. Not surprisingly, Jayne Morris is one of them.

Well-being, wisdom, wonder, and giving. *Burnout to Brilliance* embodies the essence of the fourth pillar of the Third Metric as a manifestation of the transformative power of sharing one's experience and wisdom with the world.

In *Thrive*, Arianna tells readers that one of her favorite phrases is *solvitur ambulando*—"It is solved by walking." It refers to the fourth-century-BC Greek philosopher Diogenes's response to the question of whether motion is real. To answer, he got up and walked.

As it turns out, there are many problems for which walking is the solution. In our culture of overwork, burnout, and exhaustion, how to we tap into our creativity, our wisdom, our capacity for wonder? *Solvitur ambulando.*

I encourage you to walk with Jayne Morris through the pages of this book as she guides us toward a life of brilliance.

Carla Buzasi
Editor-in-Chief of The Huffington Post UK & Global Editorial Director for HuffPost Lifestyle

Preface

Burnout is not a new phenomenon. The term was first coined in the 1960s when Graham Greene wrote the novel, *A Burn-Out Case*, telling the story of a famous architect suffering from the effects of overwork. A few years later, *burnout* was adopted as a psychological term by clinical psychologist Herbert Freudenberger.

In the 1970s Freudenberger conducted a comprehensive study and wrote about the physical signs, behaviour indicators and phases of burnout. Social psychologist Christina Maslach also studied burnout in the 1970s, devising the Maslach Burnout Inventory as a means for measuring how burnout affects workers.

At the time when this preliminary research into burnout was conducted, digital technology was still in its infancy, and there were arguably fewer contributing stressors present. With the advent of the 24/7 age of connectivity in which we now live, however, burnout has become a global cause for concern.

One of the primary reasons for this widespread increase is due to digital overload. Technological advances have certainly helped us move forward and make remarkable progresses that would not otherwise have been possible, but at the same time technology is causing many more workers to stay chained to their desks for many more hours than ever before.

A recent study[1] found that one in ten Britons now eats three meals per day at work because of such long hours and spends at least five hours and forty minutes completely desk-bound. Sitting for extended periods increases the risk of cardiovascular disease, diabetes, depression and obesity.[2] Researchers have also found that working more than eight hours per day increases the risk of dementia later in life.[3]

Neuroscientists increasingly warn us that we are consuming too much information, which causes the brain to function in a continuously hyper alert state, making it difficult to disconnect even after we manage to detach ourselves from our addictive electronic devices and switch them off.

Laptop computers, smart phones and other hand held electronic devices have begun to blur the boundaries between work and leisure. Being constantly connected to each other and to our work can result in connectivity overwhelm unless we consciously choose to unplug.

While technology has made it easier for many of us to work from anywhere in the world as long as we have an internet or telephone connection, it has made it more difficult for us to stop our work from spilling over into our family and recreation time. A study[4] published in July 2012 found that the average UK worker puts in more than three weeks of overtime a year just by answering calls and emails at home.

Unhealthy work habits are fast becoming the norm in many countries worldwide. In the UK alone during 2011-2012, almost half a million people reported suffering work related stress.[5] Across Europe work-related stress has aroused growing interest, and since 2000 there has been a noticeable increase in the level of mental health problems.

A study conducted by the European Foundation for the Improvement of Living and Working Conditions found that the UK, Greece, Ireland, Germany and Austria were the countries deemed most prevalent in terms of having high levels of work-related stress and high job demands.

Across the pond statistics are equally high,[6] with approximately 36% of American workers suggesting that they typically feel tense or stressed out during their working day. In Australia this figure is 30%, or if the 26-35 age bracket is isolated, it is much higher at 43%.

Long work weeks are often expected by employees working for a small business start-up, but in many established organisations, putting in 100 hours per week is commonplace too.

Investment bankers and PR executives are among those expected to work long hours because such practice has become entrenched in their company culture.

Short-term stress at work can be beneficial because it is thought that small secretions of stress hormones can increase your memory.[7] However, the reality for many is that working hours are increasing and stress is becoming a long-term experience leading to extreme depletion of the adrenal and autoimmune systems, eventually resulting in burnout.

In the teaching profession a study conducted by TesConnect in 2012 revealed that teachers are among the hardest working professionals in the country. The poll found that almost half of all teachers spend more time preparing lessons than they spend teaching and as much as 78% spent time on Sundays planning work for the following week.

Another study carried out by Schoolzone and Teachers Assurance in March 2013 highlighted that all participants identified themselves as feeling stressed with over 70% rating themselves at five or over on a seven-point scale. Eighty-three percent of teachers said that they felt constantly tired.

During October 2013 I was a panelist for a teacher network discussion on the topic of managing teacher stress on behalf of the *Guardian*, the world's leading liberal newspaper. One of the key concerns highlighted by the majority of teachers who took part was how to overcome the culture of overwork in schools. Many expressed that their workload was so unrelenting they were barely able to break to visit the toilet let alone to eat lunch. Continuous monitoring was highlighted as another factor contributing to high stress levels.

It has long been thought that extended holidays somewhat make up for the additional hours worked by teachers, but what about those working in organisations where there is limited holiday allowance or where employees feel too pressured by their work commitments to take their full allocation of leave?

In her book *Lean In*, Sheryl Sandberg refers to a discussion she had with Larry Kanarek, who managed the McKinsey & Company office in Washington D.C. Larry said he had noticed that employees were choosing to leave the organisation for 'one reason only: they were burnt out, tired of working long hours and travelling' and that 'all the people who quit – every single one – had unused vacation time'.

In several Western countries patterns of overwork are emerging in both public and private sectors. Fatigue is not limited to those working behind a desk. Long working hours have become a concern in the airline, rail and bus industries where strict regulations are now in place for pilots and drivers that prevents exceeding maximum hours and endangering the lives of others.

Despite the introduction of such regulations, regular accidents continue to make public news. For example, following the report of two pilots sleeping at the controls of a flight from London to New Zealand in September 2013, an investigation found that 84% of pilots felt their abilities had been 'compromised' by fatigue at some stage in the last six months. The same survey revealed that 56% of pilots admitted to napping mid-flight, with 29% saying that when they woke up, they found their co-pilot asleep too.

Overwork in hospitals is also a serious problem. In the UK, a recent investigation revealed that many physicians often work over 100 hour in a week. The extreme fatigue reported by doctors as a result risks both the lives of the medical staff and their patients.

Medical errors resulting from fatigue and subsequent investigations in the US also reveal the ramifications of the seemingly impossible workloads of medical residents. A sixteen-hour mandate was introduced in attempt to improve the situation, but a study of 2323 medical interns conducted in March 2011 found that junior doctors had more concerns about making serious medical errors after the directive was introduced than before.[8] Their hours may have been reduced, but their workloads stayed much the same, meaning they had to try to do the same amount of work in fewer hours.

The growing culture of overwork is becoming increasingly endemic and is not just a problem in the UK, USA, or Australia. I spent three years living in Japan and experienced firsthand how excessive work hours are expected of both male and female workers in jobs of all types.

For Japan, this issue has become a notable cause for concern, with around 10,000 people dying each year from what they call 'Karoshi' – literally translated as death from overwork.

In China the number of workers dying each year from exhaustion is even higher at 600,000.[9]

It has been estimated that the UK workforce are doing the equivalent to two billion hours of unpaid overtime each year[10], which is equal to one million full time jobs. The danger of allowing this trend to go unchecked is that we also start to experience an increase in fatalities occurring as a result.[11] This may sound extreme, but it is the harsh reality.

We are fast turning from a race of human 'beings' into human 'doings.' Our quality of life and our health is suffering as a result. Admitting that we cannot keep up the pace is part of the problem. It is easy to ignore warning signs and symptoms in the form of illnesses and ailments, but if we ignore them the outcome can be catastrophic.

Young workers are just as much at risk of death from overwork as their more senior colleagues. In May 2013, a twenty-four-year-old Chinese man named Li Yuan (an employee of advertising agency Ogilvy and Mather in Beijing) suffered a heart attack after staying at the office until 11pm every night for a month.

In August 2013, the death of Moritz Erhardt, a twenty-one-year-old German banking intern working for the Bank of

America's wealth management division, died unexpectedly. Merrill Lynch brought the issue to public attention internationally. Although the exact circumstances around his death are unclear, he had been working incredibly long hours and suffered a seizure after working until 6am three days in a row. Other similar stories have since started to emerge, shining a spotlight on the "churn 'em and burn 'em" cult of professionals striving to get ahead by working long hours.

A stress survey conducted in August 2013 by the Police Federation in the UK revealed that more than half of West Midlands police constables confessed wanting to quit their job due to emotional exhaustion and burnout. The study identified several key contributing factors which included high pressure peak times occurring with increased frequency, irregular breaks, inadequate facilities for breaks and intense pace of work.

Similar external pressures trigger burnout for many people; however this is often accompanied by a strong internal ambition to be extremely successful and give the outward appearance of being super human or super important.

Joan C Williams, Professor of Law at the University of California refers to the culture of overwork as the 'cult of busy smartness'. She believes that being overworked has become a socially acceptable part of our collective conditioning because we equate busyness with status:

How do the elite signal to each other how important they are? 'I am slammed' is a socially acceptable way of saying 'I am important'.

Founder of the *Huffington Post*, Arianna Huffington has talked openly about the revelation she experienced when she collapsed one day at her desk as a result of exhaustion and broke her cheekbone. The incident prompted her to challenge the concept of 'burnout as a badge of honor'. She created a campaign called *The Third Metric* to help redefine success beyond the illusive goals of obtaining wealth and power. Her work in this area hopes to raise awareness of the fact that if someone is 'working 24/7, they can't be any good. Because nobody can be any good working 24/7'.

BBC TV Presenter Andrew Marr also experienced a moment of enlightenment when he nearly lost his life due to the effects of overwork. He made his first television appearance in April 2013 after suffering a stroke early into the new year and shared publicly that he had 'been very, very heavily overworking' the year prior to his experience and was 'frankly lucky to be alive'.

In a brave, emotional interview with the *Daily Mail* newspaper, Marr shared that overwork must have been a key contributory factor to his stroke:

I was working too hard. No one made me do it, that's just the way I am… I'm a gulper, a gobbler-down of life. I wolf experiences down and, that year, I pushed my body and my mind too hard and far.

Interviews with colleagues and friends of the late Moritz Erhardt[12] have revealed that despite the bank expecting 'crazy hours' from their interns and employees, Erhardt was also self-driven to be hard working because 'he wanted to be the best'. A former classmate who attended the prestigious University of Michigan's Ross School of Management with Erhardt said that he was 'always presenting his work early, handing in projects ahead of time'.

In an online profile detailing his skills and career ambitions, Erhardt said that from a young age he had a 'persistent aspiration' to be good at everything. He wrote:

I have grown up in a family that expected me, in whatever respect, to excel in life. By implication, I felt somehow pressurized… However, I did not intend to belie my parents' expectations. Therefore, I have become a highly competitive and ambitious nature from early on... Already during my times in elementary school, I began playing soccer as well as tennis, I engaged in track and field athletics, and I started ski racing. Sometimes, I had a tendency to be over-ambitious, which resulted in severe injuries.... With respect to my performance in school, I was striving for excellence and trying to be the best all the time.

Burnout cannot be blamed entirely on the heavy workloads and the expectations that organisations place on their employees. Undeniably there are several workplace stressors that can lead to burnout, but for the majority of individuals caught up in burning the candle at both ends, it is their internal drivers and ambitions coupled with societal and technological stressors that eventually lead to burnout.

In order to address the issue, both organisations and individuals need to take responsibility for solving the situation and devising strategies for sustainable success. The exercises I have included within this book are designed to help you break old burnout habits and shift your mindset so that you can better cope with external challenges.

It is also my intention to challenge our unhealthy global work culture and contribute towards collective change. I feel passionately about bringing balance back to business so that people can pursue their passions and purpose whilst achieving optimum health, wealth and well-being.

Introduction

Are you burning out? If you routinely run on reserves and force yourself to accept that constantly feeling tired is all part and parcel of living a busy life, then you – like millions of others – are probably wondering if you are ever going to find a way to escape the exhaustion.

When the signs and symptoms of stress go beyond inconvenient headaches, disturbed sleep or difficulty concentrating and result in the prescription of pills to treat prolonged complaints, then it's truly time to listen to your body and commit to making change. If, like many of my clients, you feel that putting up with the pain and struggle is no longer an option, then this book will help you transform your life from burnout to brilliance as you develop your own strategies for sustainable success.

Burnout Defined

Burnout has become a universally accepted term; it seems to be thrown around somewhat interchangeably with the term 'stress'. This causes confusion as to what burnout really means and who it affects.

Some argue that various lifestyles can lead to burnout, suggesting that it can equally affect the university student, single parent, self-employed or an alternating shift worker. Others insist that it is specific to highflying executives or leaders of large organisations. In the business context there is also disagreement when it comes to the primary cause of burnout, some placing onus on organisations and others suggesting that the individual alone is responsible.

More specifically, burnout is the result of various factors cumulating in prolonged stress and poor lifestyle choices that lead to severe depletion of the autoimmune system and adrenal glands. It is not unique to one type of personality or profession, but in all burnout cases many common underlying factors can be found. Burnout as a phenomenon is increasingly affecting people from various backgrounds.

Each burnout experience is unique to the individual. Some people completely crash, while others repeat patterns of chronic self-destruction throughout the course of their life, continuously feeling run-down yet never actually reaching breaking point.

Burnout impacts us not just as individuals but also heavily drains our organisations and depletes our economies due to the unprecedented costs on our medical and social support systems.[13] It has recently become a global cause for concern because it is an unsustainable framework upon which we are subconsciously building the future of our planet.

However, burnout can be transformed into an opportunity for us, individually and collectively, to harness our full potential and productivity. In order for this transformation to happen we need to learn how to listen to, respect and trust our intuition and the wisdom of our bodies.

If you identify with overwhelming feelings of exhaustion and overload, then this book will help you explore the combination of internal drivers and external factors contributing towards the creation of your experience.

This book is not just about helping you recognise signs of burnout so you can understand the causes. It will also help you uncover and release any associated guilt or shame and effectively challenge the social stigma surrounding burnout.

In a society addicted to success and competitiveness we are encouraged to exceed expectations in every area of our lives. Admitting burnout can therefore feel like admitting failure for both individuals and organisations that foster conditions contributing towards this problem.

When we reframe burnout as a powerful paradigm for self-inquiry and development, it is possible to tap into phenomenal personal learning and the opportunity for transformational change.

How to Use This Book

This book is divided into three distinct sections: Discovery, Recovery and Brilliance. At the end of each, you will find a 'Need-to-Know' executive summary of key points. I have included this feature for the following three reasons:

1. I know you are busy. The summary pages mean you can glance ahead and quickly and easily gain an overview of the whole book and start benefiting from the essence of the contents immediately. It is okay to jump ahead. By skimming the book before properly reading it, your conscious mind begins to process thoughts and reflections, which then deepen your overall experience when revisiting each chapter.

2. Reading the summary sections at the end of each part of the book will help to reinforce your learning.

3. You can use the summary pages to reference key points and dip back in and out of the book as and when you desire.

We all learn and process information differently. As such, in addition to this book, I have created an accompanying webpage with videos, podcasts and printable worksheets. I encourage you to visit the site to maximise your multi-sensory learning experience of the material contained in this book: www.jaynemorris.com.

PART 1 – DISCOVERY

Identifying Signs and Symptoms

In August 2013 I participated in a panel discussion titled 'Modern Living: Less Stress, More Living' at the *Wilderness Festival*, deep in the Oxfordshire countryside. The conversation was hosted by the Global Director of Huffington Post Lifestyle and Editor-in-Chief, Carla Buzasi. The hot topic of discussion was how to press the pause button on our addiction to busy-ness and avoid stress and burnout.

With me on the panel was Ruby Wax, an American comedian, writer and mental health campaigner. In her book *Sane New World*, Wax states:

> *Learning how to self-regulate means you can sense the early warnings before a full on burnout or depression and do something about it.*

If you can sense the early warning signs you can avoid burnout completely. In fact, I believe is even *easy* to spot and stop burnout, when you know how. The problem is that when you get stuck being a slave to busy-ness it can be difficult to pause and stay still long enough to reflect because you are so pre-occupied with your struggle to survive.

Burnout can seemingly appear from nowhere and trap us like quick sand. It can cause us to sink deeper and deeper into an experience of overwhelm, stress and exhaustion. As this happens, not only are we drowning ourselves but also drowning out the voices of those around us who are trying to help. We can't hear them. We can't hear ourselves.

And yet, in our darkest moment, in the very depths of despair, the still quiet voice of inner wisdom is always present and can still be heard.

Sharon Hensall, editor of *Inspired Times Publications,* recalls how burnout made her feel like a slave to her mind. When her body started to shut down; however, she finally chose to listen and found the guidance she needed in order to turn things around:

Looking back it amazes me that I survived that period of my life as I clocked up 100 hours of work some weeks and was living on four hours' sleep a night. There was too much pressure in all aspects of life. I was always pushing myself to work harder rather than accepting if things weren't achievable in 'normal' hours then maybe it wasn't sustainable. I was so stuck in patterns of burnout that I found I was unable to step back from the situation and find a solution. Because I felt so overwhelmed at the time I simply couldn't seem to see any way out that didn't involve more hard work.

My health, both physical and mental suffered... I began to feel an exhaustion so deep that it scared me. Slowly my mind felt it was clouding over, I no longer could remember all I needed to do and needed to make note of everything to ensure mistakes wouldn't be made. My body was starting to buckle. I felt I was dragging my body through the day – as though I was climbing mountains even when walking downhill. There was an awareness rising that my lifestyle wasn't sustainable. I began to feel defeated – not something I'd ever felt before.

I felt obsessed with sleep but no matter how much I got, I felt exhausted – my dreams were intense and exhausting so I never felt rested the next morning. My muscles hurt – my whole body hurt in fact. I felt out of breath from any slight exertion. My memory was poor and I couldn't retain any information for more than a few seconds. I felt overwhelmed and when alone, overcome with emotion and depleted. I felt as if my life force was running out. The doctors said I was low in iron and an herbalist felt my symptoms were that of adrenal fatigue.

I felt that my only hope was to clear my mind and see things differently. I booked on a retreat. I felt it was my only hope to clear my mind. I had an epiphany whilst on the retreat – I reached a deeper understanding of how I'd created this situation. I saw that my approach had brought on my burnout. I never let up – I'd lost my connection with the truth of each moment and had created a mountain in my mind, which needed climbing each day to reach perfection. I over-complicated things as I felt that I needed to achieve so much to satisfy my own expectations, which were actually impossible.

I now listen to my body and deeper instincts – approaching each day with a manageable amount to do and rest when I need it. I no longer feel a slave to my mind.

We all have an internal voice of wisdom and intuition. It acts as a guidance system to help maintain balance of body, mind and soul. It nudges us gently toward the things that are aligned with our highest good.

Are you willing to listen?

Intuition can come in the form of ideas that suddenly appear in your thoughts, in images in your dreams, as whispers of your inner voice, or as sensations in your body indicating that something feels instinctively *right* or *wrong*. It also shows up when we feel drawn to certain people, places and things and repelled by others.

Our internal thoughts, emotions, energy and external experiences are intrinsically linked. Metaphysical messages signaling that we are burning out can come through both our internal and external environments.

As we go about our day-to-day lives, guidance can show up as images or pictures that we see in magazines, on posters or on the TV. It can be heard in the lyrics of music or words that jump out in conversations. It can also present itself during the apparent coincidence of certain events that on some unexplained level a deeper part of our inner knowing interprets as somehow being symbolic.

Whenever our body is exposed to stress we receive whispers

of guidance accompanied by mild physical symptoms like a headache, sore back, difficulty sleeping, tiredness, dizziness or indigestion problems. These signs are designed to help us slow down and bring things back into balance in our lives.

In the western world we often suppress these warning signs by self-medicating without exploring the root cause. Instead of pausing to explore the reason for having a headache or backache and treating the root cause, we often choose to pop a pill and carry on.

When we override such signs then the body starts to shout for us to pay attention by sending more serious conditions like cancer, a heart attack or stroke.

One of my first experiences of recognising this mind-body connection occurred back in 2007 when I worked with an incredible woman named Jenny[14] who, in addition to accepting a role on the board for the law firm that she worked for, was also raising three children as a single parent and attempting to provide care for her elderly father who had recently taken ill. She said it was as if she had been 'carrying the weight of the world on her shoulders'.

Jenny had become accustomed to functioning under pressure; as long as she kept herself busy she felt she could keep going at an incredible pace. Jenny said that her intuition was telling her to lessen her load, but instead she was choosing to try keep doing it all. As a result she started to experience depression, which she said felt like an overwhelming pressure that she just could not shift.

In our sessions together we explored the root cause beliefs underlying Jenny's compulsion to take on so much responsibility. We also looked at some of the changes that Jenny could make in her life that would help to reduce the pressure. She came up with creative ways to delegate some of the things she had previously been struggling to handle alone. After a few days she reported feeling 'lighter, brighter, and more confident in coping with everything at work and at home'. Her depression disappeared. When we heal our minds, we heal our bodies. We will explore this in more detail in the second section of the book, *Recovery*.

Emotional and Cognitive Symptoms

When humans experience ongoing stress, our physiological functions (e.g., sleep, learning and memory) are affected by our thoughts, emotions and memories. This can result in memory problems, the experience of depression, anxiety disorders, labyrinthitis (extreme dizziness), low libido, mental exhaustion, insomnia, persistent restlessness, feelings of overwhelm, moodiness, loneliness, the inability to relax, recurrent dreams, difficulty concentrating, reduced judgment, constant worrying, and can even accelerate brain aging.

These symptoms negatively affect our general behaviour and health choices. When we are chronically stressed we can become more sensitive to criticism, lose our sense of humor and develop nervous tendencies. We are more likely to make poor dietary choices, eat too much or too little, and become dependent on caffeine and other stimulants, in addition to seeking alcohol, cigarettes or other drugs to help us relax.

Depression

In my work with people overcoming burnout I have met many people (like Jenny) who suffer from depression. Not everyone who experiences burnout experiences the same symptoms, so not everyone who burns out can relate to depression, but many people report sensations of persistent sadness or feelings of worthlessness and helplessness that are typically associated with depression.

We all have days where we just don't feel right and no matter what we do, no matter how positively we think, we just feel rotten. When this is ignored, it can continue and eventually lead to the experience of depression.

According to the World Health Organisation more than 350 million people worldwide suffer from some form of depression. British workers are the most depressed in Europe according to the Impact of Depression in the Workplace in Europe Audit conducted in 2012.

Jeff Foster, author of *The Deepest Acceptance*, who himself journeyed through depression, points out that the verb has the similar phonetic sound as 'deep rest' . He believes that depression is a hidden invitation to release the pressure of being someone you are not so that you can 'rest deeply in the core of who you are'.

As is the case with many challenges in life, including depression, I find that 'what you resist, persists', and that accepting and exploring a difficult situation ultimately allows us to reconnect with our true passions and purpose and be renewed.

I have been incredibly moved by the story of Beverley Jones, one of my clients, who credits several techniques that I will be sharing in this book for helping her to shift old patterns of doing too much and trying to be everything to everyone. Beverley experienced physical and emotional signs in the form of panic attacks and depression, which she spent years overriding until her body eventually forced her to stop.

Beverley reported feeling like a failure when she faded from being her 'strong, able, resilient and confident' former self into a 'crying, de-energised, angry, negative person' who felt 'useless and pathetic'.

Her breakthrough came when she found the strength to reach out for help, which began with going to see her physician. With the support of antidepressants, counseling and coaching, Beverley gradually rebuilt her confidence and her life. After attending a vision board[15] workshop that I led in 2011, she said her thinking was 'moved to another level' as she 'was taken down another avenue' of her journey and 'literally walked away' with her 'future in (her) hands'.

Beverley wrote about her journey through burnout and her experience of depression in her book titled *Made It Thru the Rain*, a brave account of how she learned to listen to her body and rediscovered the powerful person who resided within.

Anxiety

Statistics indicate that anxiety disorders have soared internationally since the credit crunch. In the UK the number of people being treated for anxiety more than quadrupled between 2006/2007 and 2010/2011.[16] In the USA anxiety disorders have become the most common mental illness suffered by adult Americans today.

Anxiety is commonly triggered by stress, usually presenting itself in response to external events or circumstances. It can also surface as a result of internal fears and habitual negative thinking. For many people it can come unexpectedly, in response to positive as well as negative life changes, and at any age and stage.

Common physical symptoms associated with anxiety include excessive sweating, nausea, diarrhoea, irritability, frequent urination, disturbed sleep, headaches or trembling. These symptoms can be annoying when you want to create the impression of being as cool as a cucumber. Medication can help to mask the symptoms but not to address the root of the issue.

Some psychiatrists believe that too many people are being prescribed medication such as Prozac and Valium to help them cope with feelings and anxieties that are considered quite normal responses to financial worries or work-related stresses:

The pharmaceutical industry is always looking for new markets, and anxiety disorder is increasingly the diagnosis given to people who are distressed and upset. GPs don't have time to talk to patients about why they are really unhappy; it is easier to treat situations as a standard disorder.

Dr Joanna Moncrieff, Consultant Psychiatrist

If you feel that anxiety is preventing you from functioning properly in normal day-to-day situations or is manifesting itself as a physical ailment(s), then it is important to seek medical advice.

Severe anxiety can be debilitating and requires professional help. Be sure to ask your doctor what kind of psychological counseling or other talking therapies and stress management programmes are available to you in addition to exploring medical treatments. Speaking with someone can make a big difference. There are many psychotherapeutic, coaching, yoga and meditation-based exercises and actions that you can take to help you overcome and avoid general anxiety.

Mild anxiety is often experienced as a state of overall concern about confronting common work/life challenges like taking a test, delivering a speech or meeting the in-laws for the first time. This level of anxiety may cause feelings of nervousness, worry and apprehension.

Shortly after her rise to fame as a popular author, J.K. Rowling publicly reported experiencing anxiety in response to struggling with what she likened to a 'tsunami of demands'. She said that the experience felt overwhelming, as if she had to solve everyone's problems. In order to help her cope, Rowling sought therapy, which she said helped a great deal.

Some of the most outwardly successful people I have worked with have sought my expertise to help them face their fears and control anxiety. I use a combination of life coaching, martial arts, meditation and art psychotherapy techniques to help people identify the root cause of their concerns, confront their challenges, breathe through their worries, replace negative talk with positive affirmations, visualise themselves experiencing successful outcomes and prioritise sufficient rest and relaxation.

Many of these techniques are within this book.

Top 5 Tips to Increase Your Sense of Inner Calm and Confidence:

1. **Remember to breathe:** One of the main symptoms of anxiety is shallow breathing. Whenever you feel overwhelmed, stop whatever you are doing and go to a window or get outside. (Close your eyes or gaze into space if for any reason you are in a situation where you can't do this.) Turn your focus to your breathing. Take three full deep breaths, inflating your stomach like a baby as you breathe in. Notice your breath filling your lungs completely as you breathe in. Listen to your breath as you exhale slowly and completely. Spend a few moments concentrating only on your breathing. With each further breath hold the thought: 'I am breathing in peace'. And with each next out breath hold the thought: 'I am breathing out tension'. This will instantly help to reoxygenate and renergise your blood cells and bring an associated sense of calm and increased well-being.

2. **Flip your negative thoughts**: Begin to notice your self-talk, the little things you repeat to yourself each day, and ask yourself whether they are positive or negative. If they are negative try and flip them to create more empowering positive phrases. Repeat these new phrases to yourself instead. By doing this you are literally retraining your brain to think positively, overcome anxiety and achieve success in all areas of your life.

3. **Feel your fear:** I earlier noted the phrase, 'what you resist, persists'. Acknowlege your fear by giving it a means of expressing itself rather than supressing or fighting it,

which will only make it worse. Try shouting all your frustration into a pillow, shaking your whole body to discharge your nervous tembles or tensing up all of your muscles as tightly as you can, from the top of your head all the way to the tips of your toes, hold for a few moments, then instantly release and feel your tension melt away.

4. **Smile from the inside:** A positive attitude is contagious. Start by imagining a big smile inside your stomach that grows to fill your whole body. Notice how your face wants to smile as a response. Allow your face to smile. Now focus on a positive thought that will energise and uplift you today. Return to it anytime you need a boost.

5. **Visualise success:** Instead of focusing on the worst case scenario, try visualising the best outcome that you could possibly have. Play a video in your mind's eye of you calmly and confidently overcoming your challenge, feel the sensations of success flowing through your body, and hear the responses of those around you supporting you. You hold the power to make it your reality. Replay it often!

Tearfulness

Burnout takes its toll on our emotions. Increased tearfulness is often a sign that you have taken on too much. As you work through the exercises in this book there may be moments when you feel the urge to cry. I encourage you to allow your tears to flow. Crying is a perfectly natural and healthy way of expressing and releasing emotion for both men and women.

Although tears can be created purely as a reflex reaction to something blowing in our eyes or the scent of an onion, they are also shed as part of complex neurophysiological process enabling us to connect with and process a range of emotions including joy, frustration, stress, anger, sadness, hurt and pain.

Women are genetically more likely to cry than men because we produce higher levels of the emotional tear-inducing hormone prolactin. There is, however, no difference between how men and women cry, other than our interpretation of what is acceptable.

Both men and women can feel uncomfortable shedding tears, especially in the workplace, because from an early age we are conditioned that to succeed in business we must 'stay strong', hide our vulnerabilities and never expose weakness.

Our resistance to crying in front of others is likely to stem from our primal instinct to protect ourselves against predators because in nature tears tend to be interpreted as a signal of distress or helplessness. Yet in exposing our vulnerability we access the power of authentic self-expression and communication, which can be our greatest strength.

Howard Schultz of Starbucks grew what began as a Seattle coffeeshop in 1987 into a global retail powerhouse by the early 2000s. Schultz then left his position as CEO and took a break from the business for eight years. During that time Starbucks slipped into slow demise and found itself in deep water. Howard was brought back in to turn things around.

Instead of putting on a brave face he allowed himself to be open and honest. In a meeting with the company's global management he wore his heart on his sleeve and wept as he poured out how deeply he cared about the employees and their families, which he felt he had failed. By making himself vulnerable and speaking the truth of how he felt about the situation, he roused the support of the entire company. It was the middle of a recession, yet within two years Starbucks succeeded in transforming performance and went on to deliver its highest revenue and earnings.

Expressing our emotions is important for making a deeper level of connection with colleagues in the work place, but crying has other benefits too. Crying provides us with a natural coping mechanism for the build-up of stress because it helps us to release stress and toxins from our system and experience the euphoria of endorphins that stimulate relaxation and promote the renewal and restoration of our internal organs.

When we try to suppress stress and emotion the cumulative effect often leads to experiences of overwhelm, stress and ill health. Crying calms us and provides a cleansing detox for the mind, body and soul. For men and women caught up burning the candle at both ends, crying is a restorative way to help return balance and prevent adrenal fatigue.

In this moment and at any time you feel tears welling up inside you, be brave enough to connect with your true feelings, face your greatest fears, acknowledge your most sincere longings, rediscover your sense of passion and purpose and give yourself permission to be truly powerful.

Cry. Forgive. Learn. Move on. Let your tears water the seeds of your future happiness.
Steve Maraboli

Recurring Dreams

When we sleep our subconscious mind processes thoughts and emotions and accesses inner guidance. Symbols are the language of our dreams, and deciphering them can help you discover deeper understanding, enabling you to apply learning across all areas of your life. Recurring dreams signal messages we most need to interpret. Understanding your dreams can help you learn more about your experience of burnout.

There is no one more suited to interpreting your dreams than yourself. Try keeping a pad of paper, some pens and crayons next to your bed. When you begin to stir, write or draw whatever you are able to remember from your dreams. Ask yourself: 'What are the key feelings I experienced during my dream?', 'What do these feelings remind me of?', 'Where in my life am I also experiencing these feelings?', 'If I knew what these feelings represented for me, what might their hidden message be?' Write the first answers that come to you. You may also wish to seek the assistance of someone trained in dream interpretation to help you explore this.

Insomnia

Over 51% of us find it hard to switch off and get a good night's sleep,[20] so if you have been suffering with insomnia, you are not alone. Insomnia is a sign of being unable to switch off due to overthinking and overdoing. This is a common complaint for many of my clients when they first seek my support.

People tell me time and time again that the last thing they tend to do before turning out their light to sleep is check for messages, email and Twitter or Facebook updates on their phones. This is the worst mistake you can make if you find it hard to sleep because it encourages your mind to continue being busy at the very time when it wants to unwind.

It is not only the quality of our sleep that can suffer due to overuse of our phones, our sex lives can suffer too. A recent study in the US[21] showed that 57% of women would forgo the opportunity to make love to their partners in order to continue using their phones.

Another study suggests that British women similarly hamper their sex lives because of Smartphone obsession.[22] The survey investigated the bedtime habits of 1,700 Britons and shockingly found that more than 60% of women and half of all men checked their phones during sex.

Loss of libido is a common symptom of burnout. Taking your Smartphone to bed with you only exacerbates this. If you want to rekindle your love life and get better sleep, then buy yourself a silent clock for your bedroom so that you have no reason for bringing your phone upstairs with you when you go to bed.

Make bedtime pamper time.

There are many natural remedies that can help you relax and unwind at bedtime like calming herbal teas, lavender bath salts and essential oils. But, if you feel like you've tried everything and are still not having any success try following my **Top Tips for Restful Sleep**:

Keep your bedroom clutter free – lots of clothes lying around waiting to be washed, piles of paperwork scattered on the floor or shoes strewn everywhere mean that when you climb into bed your mind is distracted by the chaos. Your bedroom needs to be a place of peace and tranquility for you to truly gain good rest.

Turn down the temperature – Studies have shown that the ideal temperature for sleeping is 15-20°C (60-68 Fahrenheit). Research also indicates that interestingly many insomniacs experience an increase in body temperature at night compared to normal sleepers and therefore struggle to fall asleep if the room is too hot. Try turning down the heat.

Keep a journal and a pen by your bed and write down everything playing on your mind before you try to nod off to sleep. It is easier to drift off without 'to do' lists floating around in your head. Get your thoughts down on paper so you can release them from your mind.

Draw a picture – you might not have played with coloured chalks or pastels since you were a child, but give yourself permission to doodle in any way you please before bed and your subconscious mind will thank you for it. Choose whatever colours you feel drawn to and allow them to swirl, twirl and make patterns on the page. This gives your subconscious the chance to process any unfinished business from your day and settle down for sleep.

Notice your thoughts – it is impossible to stop thinking completely, in fact doing this will only mean you think even more! Instead, after completing steps 1-4, notice any remaining thoughts as they come in, allow them to float by like clouds in the sky, observe them as they meander along, then just as easily allow them to float away again. Keep doing this, and before you have realised it, you will have drifted off into a deep slumber.

Physical Symptoms

Our body is excellent at communicating with us when we need to change our approach with something in our life. It gives us signs by presenting illnesses representing the root cause thinking we are holding or emotions we are suppressing. Sandy Newbigging, creator of the *Mind Detox Method*, explains this phenomenon in his powerful book, *Heal the Hidden Cause*:

> *Unhealthy beliefs can manifest physically as an unhealthy body – Beliefs have been found to have the power to influence many aspects of a person's physical functioning, including digestion, immune system, blood pressure and even DNA. Your beliefs become your biology.*

I have found that the majority of physical illnesses experienced by my clients who experience burnout stem from their tendency to consciously and sub-consciously seek out stressful situations.

Physical and emotional stress stimulates the central nervous system, in a similar way to some recreational drugs, creating the experience of a natural high. According to addiction specialist Jim Pfaus,[17] 'stressors can also wake up the neural circuitry underlying wanting and craving – just like drugs do'.

Although stressful situations may give us an enjoyable short-term buzz, our bodies are not designed to handle excessive stress on an ongoing basis.

In stressful situations when we override our intuition to rest, restore and replenish our bodies and force ourselves to run on reserves, we continuously trigger our primitive fight-or-flight response. This response has helped us handle stress since the days when our ancestors lived in caves and had to fight off or escape the attack of wild animals.

In the modern western world the threat of wild animals is no longer present, but our mind and body continue to handle stress by activating the same physiological response. Our brain therefore registers our boss yelling or the approach of a work deadline as if it were a lion – releasing adrenaline, noradrenaline and cortisol into the blood stream to help prepare our body to run or fight.

While this response helps us to be mentally alert and focus on problems at work, it can be counter-productive because we are often unable to exert ourselves physically in order to metabolise the corresponding surge of hormones sent to our muscles. Stress hormones build up in our bodies as a result, which can lead to adrenal fatigue linked to disorders of the autonomic nervous system and immune system, in addition to psychological and emotional problems.

This chronic cycle often continues until eventually the adrenal glands reach a point of over-fatigue and send symptoms signaling that we need to stress less, exercise, and/or get rest.

University of Stanford Professor Robert Sapolsky PhD explains that constant triggering of the stress response system can lead to severe damage of various organ systems within the body including:

- Cardiovascular system – resulting in damage to heart muscles and blood vessels.
- Digestive system – causing debilitating diseases and problems with digestion.
- Reproductive system – negatively affecting ovulation and

erectile function.

- Immune system – impairing immune defenses, resulting in more frequent, prolonged or severe cases of diseases ranging from mononucleosis to the common cold.

The body will break down under stress. If you refuse to follow the instructions from your conscious mind to retreat, back off, and unload some of the pressure, your unconscious may, paradoxically, instruct you to get sick to survive. The body says no, but the head says go. The body refuses to continue to acquiesce to the demands of the mind and, as a result, breaks down. Often an accident occurs or a set of symptoms emerges which requires rest and removal from the prolonged, imposed stress.

Dr Herbert Freudenberger

Physical symptoms to be aware of that can indicate adrenal exhaustion and lead to burnout include headaches, salt cravings, disturbed sleep, slow cold and flu recovery, excessive sweating (hyperhidrosis), cold hands and feet, irregular heartbeat, panic attacks, physical exhaustion, ovarian cysts, abnormally high/low blood pressure, low stamina, craving sweet foods, loss/partial loss of sight, carpal tunnel syndrome, RSI (repetitive strain injury), back pain, irritable bowel syndrome, allergies and respiratory problems.

When we fail to explore these symptoms and identify the corresponding root cause beliefs and suppressed emotions, our conditions can worsen resulting in the extreme dysregulation of adrenaline and cortisol in the bloodstream and diagnosis of autoimmune disorders and associated illnesses including MS, ME, chronic fatigue, lupus, post viral fatigue syndrome, hypothyroidism, fibromyalgia, rheumatoid arthritis, asthma, cardiovascular disease, diabetes and even cancer.[18]

The book *Heal Your Body* by Louise Hay is an excellent tool that I highly recommend for helping you explore the probable underlying thought processes connected with the physical conditions you may have been experiencing, in addition to new thought patterns that you can use to replace, reconnect, and heal. I will also share a variety of powerful exercises in the coming chapters to help you more deeply explore the internal thoughts that lie behind the current choices you subconsciously make on a daily basis that cumulatively effect your overall health, wealth, wellbeing and relationships.

Adrenal Fatigue

If you think your adrenal glands may be fatigued from continuously triggering the fight-or-flight response, there are three simple checks you can conduct at home, without the need for any special equipment. These tests are described by Kathryn R Simpson in her book *Overcoming Adrenal Fatigue.*[19] Although they cannot guarantee accurate results, knowledge of these tests and your body's response to them can help you present a request to your doctor for lab tests to be taken and further investigation.

In all cases, I recommend seeking medical advice for any health related concerns that you have in addition to following the exercises and activities I offer in this book.

White Line Test

Back in the early 1900s, a French doctor named Emile Sergent discovered that when someone is suffering from adrenal fatigue, the skin on the abdomen stays a white colour for approximately two minutes when scratched.

To try this test at home, take a ball point pen and turn it so that the bottom of the pen is aligned with your stomach. Pressing firmly, but not overly hard, make a mark approximately 15cm or 6 inches across your stomach.

The mark will turn from white to red within about 10 seconds if your adrenal glands are operating healthily. If you have low adrenal function the mark will remain white for a couple of minutes before returning back to normal.

Pupil Contraction Test

A common symptom of adrenal fatigue is discomfort in bright sunlight. This is because the pupils of the eyes are not able to maintain a steady contraction when there is bright light. You can test this for yourself with the help of a friend. Find a dark room and have your friend shine a flashlight past your eye. Ask them to watch to see whether your pupil contracts and stays contracted, or whether it briefly contracts, then dilates or partially dilates. Dilation indicates adrenal fatigue.

Blood Pressure Test

Another general sign of adrenal fatigue is for blood pressure to drop rather than increase when you move from sitting or lying down to a standing position. For this test you need a simple blood pressure monitor, unless you are confident checking your pulse using your fingers. Relax by lying flat for five minutes. Take your blood pressure and record the reading. Then, stand up and immediately take your blood pressure again. If your blood pressure has decreased it can indicate postural hypotension, which is a sign of adrenal fatigue.

Breakdowns

When we fail to take care of ourselves properly we can also become too tired and preoccupied to notice other areas in our lives that need our attention. The result of ignoring guidance often leads to other things in our lives breaking down, exploding, burning out, falling apart or disintegrating.

If we take notice when this happens, and explore the hidden meanings, we enable ourselves to choose what we need to make better or mend, both on the inside and out.

But if we push on regardless, further illness, accidents, breakages and breakdowns are sure to follow until we stop, rest and reevaluate.

Common Indicators

- Dead plants or flowers in your home or office
- Relationship breakdowns
- Reduced sexual intimacy with partner
- Children demonstrating behaviour problems
- Cars, appliances, central heating systems, computers and electronics breaking down due to neglect
- Clumsiness, forgetfulness, losing things
- Car accidents
- Making absentminded mistakes like leaving keys in the front door
- Cluttered home/office environment

Clutter

Clutter is what silts up exactly like silt in a flowing stream when the current, the free flow of the mind, is held up by an obstruction.
May Sarton

Clutter is often indicative of burnout. As I mentioned at the start of this chapter, our internal and external worlds are intrinsically linked.

Internally, when we have negative, fear-based or busy thinking, it accumulates and manifests as thought clutter, clogging up the flow of energy in every aspect of our lives.

Externally, our modern lifestyles are also to blame for our clutter. Statistics show we are making more purchases and accumulating more clutter in our lives than ever before. In a society that continues to support excessive production of short-lived, disposable items, it is not just our closets that are jam-packed.

Exposure to a high speed, media-intense world, coupled with compulsive multi-tasking at work and home, overloads our minds and our environment. Fast food, pollution and overstimulation taxes our bodies, while calendars bursting with tightly packed schedules burden our sense of personal space.

I often use the clutter circle diagram below to help explain to clients the far-reaching impact of their root cause burnout beliefs in addition to exploring the impact of external pressures. As you look at the diagram, try answering the following questions:

What areas of your life have become clogged up with your conscious and subconscious thought clutter?

- Physical – do you hold on to physical things you no longer need, use, love or care about?
  This includes the things you accumulate in your home, office, wallet, purse or handbags.

- Body clutter – are you carrying excess weight? Are you burdened by illnesses and ailments? Do you regularly neglect your intuition to rest, eat well or exercise? Do you over-exercise or exercise when you really need to rest? Anything you put into your body that is not supportive of you or anything you do to or with your body that is not healthful contributes to this.

- Time clutter – are you constantly running from appointment to the next? Are social media networks robbing you of rest?

  Time clutter is all the things you end up doing, committing too or being involved with that you do not really enjoy but fill your time with anyway because you get drawn into them out of habit, or overextend yourself with because you feel you should, ought to or must.

- Relationship clutter – where in your life are you experiencing relationship ruptures?

  There is a saying that people come into our lives for a reason, season or a lifetime. If you feel drained, depleted and unfulfilled from a relationship in your life, examine whether it has passed its expiry date or whether there is something more you are being challenged to explore, change and learn from.

  How is your relationship with yourself? Become aware of your self-talk – what phrases you find you often tell yourself? Notice whether they are cruel or kind, caring or overly demanding.

- Energy or spirit – do you feel knocked off, disconnected, tired, unable to switch off, generally resentful, angry or unenthusiastic?

  When this is balanced you feel a general sense of wellbeing; you are energised, all your organs are vital, you are connected with your intuition and internally guided by what you know is aligned with your own individual energy. Your energy is clear (it is not influenced by the energy of other people). Your *chi* flows with grace and ease through your energetic body without any energetic blockages.

In minds crammed with thoughts, organs clogged with toxins, and bodies stiffened with neglect, there is just no space for anything else.
Alison Rose Levy

In the next chapter I offer exercises to help you identify the conscious and subconscious thinking that has been showing up as clutter in your life and preventing you from listening to, trusting and honouring your intuition.

You can clear the clutter in your life from both the inside out and from the outside in. I will be encouraging you throughout this book to examine the clutter in every area of your life and let go wherever you notice you are holding on to things you no longer need, use or love.

When I worked with Sian Hill, a Senior Marketing Account Manager, she had recently moved into a new house, and I encouraged her to use this as the ideal opportunity to declutter. 'I donated a lot of my possessions to charity and even organised a garage sale,' Sian says. 'Freeing myself from my old clutter and an environment that wasn't serving me anymore has given me a whole new lease of life and has freed up finances to fund the courses I had been looking into.' Sian has a new motto these days. If something does not feel right she declutters without delay or feelings of guilt. 'This leaves space for positive, happy things that energise me at all times,' she claims.

Often, people are reluctant to let possessions go. For many, a feeling of comfort from possessions stems from wartime rationing when food, clothes and goods were not readily available. Underpinned by the prudent ethos of 'make do and mend', people held on to their belongings for as long as possible.

After the war, when purchasing power gradually resumed, consumption of goods became a way of defining an identity, reclaiming a lifestyle suspended by war.

Hoarding not only strains the purse but also increases the amount of extra room needed to store an ever-growing cache of goods. A continuous growth of objects can take over our homes. Chantal Cooke, co-founder of Passion for the Planet, had a whole garage full of old things she no longer needed. Following a huge clear out she converted the garage into a beautiful office space overlooking her garden. 'I donated many items to charities and locals schools, sold some on eBay and gave some away through Freecycle,' Chantal recalls. 'Clearing the garage acted as a catalyst for me to sort through things I'd accumulated in my loft too.' After decluttering, many people find renewed enthusiasm to make the most of their space.

Clearing your clutter begins by making a commitment to yourself to simply get started. Begin by clearing a small manageable space, like your sock drawer or a shelf in your kitchen. The simple act of cleaning just one shelf of one cupboard in your home can serve as a powerful metaphor for sorting out other areas of your life.

You may be feeling so overwhelmed in your life that you don't know where to begin in order to move forward.

Allow one small area to act as a catalyst for much bigger change. It is all about setting an intention and making a commitment to yourself by taking action.

You can do it. See how it feels to know you've taken that first step forward!

Your Burnout Script

Carefully watch your Thoughts, for they become your Words.
Manage and watch your Words, for they will become your Actions.
Consider and judge your Actions, for they become your Habits.
Acknowledge and watch your Habits, for they become your Values.
Understand and embrace your Values, for they become your Destiny.
Mahatma Gandhi

Each burnout experience is unique, but behind every burnout experience there are certain root cause beliefs that commonly create both the internal and external experience of every individual.

From the moment of our birth, we start to form a new life script and unconscious life plan, which are the foundations of our own unique belief system that is completely exclusive to our individual life experiences. The thoughts we begin to think about our sense of 'self' and self in relation to others begin to take shape and impact the direction of our entire lives.

A psychological framework for how this happens was created in the 1950's by psychiatrist Eric Berne, MD which he called Transactional Analysis (TA).

I believe we all have an internal guidance system, a bit like a car satellite navigation system, which can help us find the optimum route to maintain the balance of our body, mind and soul.

As babies and little children we listened well to our intuitive guidance. We were very aware of the other people and how they made us feel. When inspiration came to us we followed it, and when our bodies gave us signs that things were out of balance, we responded by letting our parents or caregivers know, trusting that they would interpret our needs for us.

When we were young, those who took care of us were doing the very best they could to give us what we needed, based on the knowledge, understanding, love and attention that they had available for us at the time. Whenever someone was well attuned to us they provided exactly what we intuitively needed.

At other times when they were distracted or experiencing stress and their ability to sense or listen to us was impaired, we did not receive what we needed. Our interpretation of our childhood experiences contributed towards the formation of our sense of 'self' and our first beliefs about trusting our self.

Every human being is born into the world without bad intentions, and with the clear, strong and unambivalent need to maintain life, to love and be loved.
Alice Miller

With reference to Berne's work, Stewart and Joines, in their book titled *TA Today*[23], suggest that at birth we begin not only developing an awareness of ourselves but that from this we construct an unconscious life plan based on our experiences, observations and interactions with others. They suggest that we fill in the details during early childhood, so that by the age of four we have 'decided on the essentials of the plot'.

Children are like wet cement. Whatever falls on them makes an impression.
Dr Haim Ginot

As poet Dorothy Law Nolte once wrote in her poem with the same title 'Children Live What They Learn'[24], the demands and expectations of our parents, care givers, teachers and other external authorities become internalised and also form part of our script.

Stewart and Joines suggest that by age seven we have completed the outline of our 'life story' and 'all its main details' and that extras are added in here and there until we reach twelve years of age, when we then start to revise the story and update it with 'more real-life characters'.

Once we reach adulthood, the beginnings of the story have left our conscious memory, yet without awareness of it, they suggest that we are 'likely to live out the story composed all those years ago'.

The script we create as children determines how we relate to ourselves and therefore also how we relate to others. The beliefs within our script steer the conscious and subconscious choices we make in life; they govern our responses to situations, circumstances and events, and ultimately influence both our internal and external experience.

Much of what we write in our internal scripts determines whether we are likely to make choices later on in life that lead to burnout, or not.

In the study of transactional analysis there are five phrases referred to as drivers that commonly become part of our script, in addition to fifteen internal commands.[25]

Internal Drivers

- Please Me (Please Someone)
- Be Perfect!
- Be Strong!
- Try Hard!
- Hurry Up!

Commands

- Don't Be (Don't Exist)
- Don't Be Who You Are
- Don't Be a Child
- Don't Grow Up
- Don't Succeed

- Don't Do Anything
- Don't Be Important
- Don't Belong
- Don't Be Close
- Don't Be Well (Don't be Sane)
- Don't Think
- Don't Feel
- Don't Leave Me
- Don't Change
- You Should or You Deserve To – have this happen in your life, so it doesn't have to happen to me.

There are elements of each driver that arguably provide us with positive resources to achieve things that may otherwise have been unobtainable; however when strong drivers are coupled with strong commands the results can be extremely detrimental to the individual.

An example of this would be someone with the driver to 'Be Perfect' alongside the command 'Don't Be a Child'. The results are likely to be someone who sets extremely high standards, works long hours to maintain perfectionism and finds it almost impossible to relax, have fun and enjoy life.

Another example would be someone with the driver 'Please Me' with the command 'Don't Feel'. The results? Someone who is forever attempting to go the extra mile for clients or customers, over and above what is necessary, in addition to trying to keep everyone happy at home. This same person would typically find it hard to say 'No' and feel incredibly guilty if physically unable to help whenever asked. He/she would also feel compelled to override signals given by their body telling them to rest if there was something still needing to be done to help or please someone else.

When we override intuition with conditioning the result is the neglect of self-care. This negatively impacts the relationship we have with our 'self', in addition to our relationships with others. The ramifications of this can have a negative knock-on effect on our finances and career advancement prospects too. Everything suffers.

I can't take care of anyone else unless I take care of myself... This is how I look at life. I have to attend to myself first in order to be spiritually, emotionally, intellectually, and physically available to others. If you have trouble with the semantics of putting yourself first, think of it as preparation to serve others.
Michael Hyatt, former CEO, Thomas Nelson Publishers

Self-care is dependent on self-awareness. As you increase awareness of your internal thought processes you in turn increase your ability to identify how your thoughts have manifested themselves in each area of your life. This enables you to regain the power to change your thinking, shift your mindset and transform your experience from one of burnout to one of brilliance.

No longer do you need to play the victim to your old thinking.

You can become the creator of your own life masterpiece.

To help you raise your own self-awareness I have created a two-minute online test. To discover your own personal burnout score go to: www.jaynemorris.com

Learning from Your Past

The outer conditions of a person's life will always be found to reflect their inner beliefs.
James Allen

The thoughts you hold determine your words and your actions. The thinking that you experienced in relation to previous events, circumstances, yourself and others in your life have shaped how you currently 'show up' in the world.

The way you experience your life tomorrow is dependent on the quality of your thinking *today*.

Changing your thoughts has the power to change your life.

When the root cause thinking that created the combination of factors leading to burnout is uncovered, it can be challenged, released and changed. This in turn has the power to transform the next chosen course of action taken, from one chartered for burnout to one aligned with brilliance.

Life Exploration Exercise

As we explored in *Your Burnout Script*, drivers, injunctions and fear have also been frequently running the show. When this happens your brilliance becomes lost and diluted. By taking a moment to reflect key thoughts, actions and life experiences you can identify the root beliefs that have kept you from trusting your internal guidance in addition to your inspired thoughts, intuitive insights and corresponding moments of brilliance.

A useful exercise to help you do this is to draw a life exploration, which is basically the journey of your life plotted out by marking down the key influential events and circumstances that had an impact on your thinking, the beliefs you formed and the decisions you have made throughout your life.

Start by taking a sheet of paper and some coloured pens. Draw a horizontal line along the very bottom of the page. At the start of the line mark '0' to represent your conception. A little further along the line mark 'birth' to represent when you were born. Next add key years of your life through to the end of the line where you can put an arrow pointing onwards in the direction of your future.

Choosing whatever colour you most feel drawn towards, begin to plot out key life experiences that you have had, using the space above the line. You can write down words and/or draw pictures. For each influential experience make a note of the key learning that you gained and what beliefs you formed in relation to the experience. Also note what thoughts, feelings and emotions you were holding prior to each event, situation or circumstance.

For example, you may have moved home when you were small and remember feeling scared or excited and forming a thought about change being frightening or exciting as a result. During primary school you may reflect on influential teachers that you had and the things they encouraged you to do, or told you not to do, and the impact that this had.

After recording as many of the key details from your life that come to mind, sit for a moment and look at your life exploration. Identify the major challenges in your life that you have overcome. Ask yourself what were the key strengths or beliefs that helped you to move through tough times.

With appreciation and gratitude make a note of all the positive personal qualities and life skills that you have gained along your journey. Become aware of the moments when you followed your gut intuition and made decisions that felt *right*.

All aspects of your journey have led you to this moment in your life. Even though you may feel physically, mentally and emotionally exhausted right now, that does not need to be your continued experience for the future.

Within you is a diamond of brilliance that has the power to shine through anything that you have disguised it with over the years. There are times when you have allowed it to shine, drawn on its strength and rested in its radiance in the past. You did it naturally as a baby and can also connect with it just as naturally right now and forever more into your future.

Often when I am working with clients to help them release old patterns they report experiencing a sensation of fear surfacing in relation to who they would be without their story.

Stories are like boxes we build around ourselves to give structure, identity, security and familiarity. We are attached to them even when they are traumatic and painful, because they feel so much part of us... However, stories also limit us; if we grow too big they suffocate us, or if the stories grow too big they squash us and prevent us from being who we really are. Recognizing that we continuously create and repeat stories is an important step towards breaking our boxes.
Jochen Encke[26]

We all have stories. One person may be stuck in a story about lack of money; another might always be talking about how she is too busy, too tired, suffering with poor health or struggling to find the right relationship.

Our stories are made up of cluttered thoughts and notions about what we feel is wrong in our lives. The people we share our lives with are used to our stories. Other people unintentionally hold us in our stories. Our stories are part of our clutter.

Our clutter in its various forms prevents us from connecting fully to our brilliance, and it also protects us from it. Why would we want to protect ourselves from being in our brilliance? Because deep down many of us are scared of our power and potential if we were brave enough to show up in the world as our true selves, without the comfort of hiding behind our story.

Who would you be without your story? We often believe that our stories keep us safe because they are predictable. When we choose to release our stories and live from our inner brilliance, we change everything.

Author Byron Katie has developed a powerful process of self-inquiry that helps people to question the key thoughts creating their stories. Her process is based on the following questions, referred to as *The Work*:

- Is it true?
- Can you absolutely know that it's true?
- How do you react, what happens, when you believe that thought?
- Who would you be without the thought?

After getting still and answering these four questions in relation to a story you have been carrying, you then turn the thought around to its opposite or opposites and find at least three specific, genuine examples of how each turnaround is true in your life. For example, *My mother should listen to me* becomes *My mother shouldn't listen to me.* How could that be true? Find three examples. Other turnarounds might be *I should listen to me* and *I should listen to my mother.*

In turning old beliefs around profound shifts happen because we often find that the turnaround thought can be equally as true as the original story we have been telling ourselves and others.

Common Limiting Beliefs

Below is a list of common limiting beliefs that clients often uncover as part of their old burnout story. Some people find that they mildly identify with almost every belief on each list, whereas others uncover one or two beliefs that powerfully resonate and are deeply engrained. Rest assured that once they have been identified, your old beliefs can be challenged and replaced – no matter how overwhelmingly many there may be or how seemingly few, yet strongly held.

The key is to be honest with yourself and acknowledge any beliefs that feel true for you. Also add any additional beliefs that you know you hold but that don't appear below.

Once you have identified your key limiting beliefs, you can start uprooting them by writing down positive, affirming opposites and experimenting with what you would like to believe in their place.

Old Relationship Beliefs

- I should put others first
- I feel guilty if I do something for myself
- I must support (insert name of family member/group)
- I have no time for my self
- I am not worthy of …
- I am no good at …
- He/she wouldn't approve if I ….
- People like me/us/my family don't do (insert activity/job)
- Life is cruel
- Life is hard
- Life is a struggle
- XXXXX is impossible for me
- I am scared of being seen
- I am scared of success
- I am scared of failure
- I am scared of the unknown
- I am scared of losing everything
- I am scared it could all go wrong
- Other people don't like me
- Other people don't approve of me
- I must keep busy
- I always need to be doing something

Old Work Beliefs

- Work = Struggle
- Work comes first
- Work must involve sacrifice
- Work must be hard
- Work must be earned
- Success must be deserved
- Success must be competed for
- Success can be taken away over night
- I can't make money doing something I love
- The kind of work I'd really like to do is not significant enough
- People doing jobs they love are either poor or got a lucky break
- Following my passion won't pay the bills
- It doesn't matter if I hate my job
- My work should pay well
- I must work for as long as it takes to get everything done
- I must work for as long as it takes to make everything perfect
- I must work for the rest of my life
- I can earn more when I put in more hours
- Good opportunities are hard to find

Old Money Beliefs

- Money is dirty
- Money does not grow on trees
- Money is in short supply
- Money is the root of all evil
- Money goes out faster than it comes in
- It is hard to hold onto money
- Rich people are seldom happy

- Rich people are greedy and dishonest
- Rich people have no privacy
- It takes too much effort to earn lots of money
- I do not deserve to earn lots of money
- Money is not spiritual
- I need lots of money to make more money
- There is a limit to how much I can earn
- Money only comes from hard work

Old Health Beliefs

- I get ill easily
- I am always tired
- I have to push through the pain
- I cannot call in sick
- I will probably get the same disease as my mother/father/grandparent when I am older
- I cannot keep up
- I do not have time to rest
- I do not have time to exercise
- I do not enjoy exercise
- I cannot afford to exercise
- Eating this (thing that is bad for me) will not make that much difference
- Just one more glass (of alcohol) will not make that much difference
- I need to eat it to keep me going (high sugar/fat/carbohydrate food)
- I need to drink to help me sleep/cope (alcohol)
- I will start my diet next week/month/year (procrastinating)
- I will exercise next week/month/year
- I am not over-exercising; I just need to complete this (marathon/race/other big challenge)

When *Hunt Big Sales* CEO Tom Searcy went through a particularly tiring period, his lack of energy nearly led to him shutting the business he loved. He recognised that he needed to figure out how to get his energy back. Upon reflection of how he got so exhausted he says:

> *Most of the fatigue that hits us as CEOs doesn't come upon us all at once. Instead, fatigue creeps up on us. The causes, I think, are common: I worry over suppliers, employees, customers, cash flow, regulation—and the fact that everything takes too *&^% long! These frustrations are pretty typical of most small and midsize companies. Even if you have a very small business with almost no staff, there are times when day-to-day concerns can wear you out.*

Are you ready to overcome your overwork habits, fight your fatigue and turn around your entire burnout story so that you can discover who you might be without it?

The following art exercise has helped many of my clients to clear their old story in preparation for writing a new, more positive and inspiring script.

Use it now to powerfully clear any thought clutter that has been blocking the brilliance of your inner diamond.

Diamond Exercise

Take a fresh piece of paper and draw a diamond at the centre. This represents the essence of you. Give yourself permission to draw the diamond imperfectly. It does not matter how accurately your picture actually resembles a diamond. All that matters is the intention you set right now to set yourself free from anything that has clogged up your thinking, energy, relationships, wealth, career, health and wellbeing.

Draw or write around the picture of your diamond any of the old thoughts that you would now like to let go of.

Just as easily as any of your previous patterns of thinking

were first formed, they can now be released. Your mind is incredibly powerful and capable of creating new neurological pathways for your thinking to follow.

Imagine you are doing some weeding in your garden. You have a lovely lawn, and you are making space for new shoots of grass to take the place of some of the moss and weeds that were quietly preventing them from coming through before.

I discovered that when I believed my thoughts, I suffered, but when I didn't believe them, I didn't suffer, and that this is true for every human being. Freedom is as simple as that. I found that suffering is optional. I found a joy within me that has never disappeared, not for a single moment. That joy is in everyone, always.
Byron Katie

Once you have finished adding all your old limited or fear based thinking to your diamond picture, draw little lines on the picture connecting all of the clutter on your picture to your diamond in the centre. These little lines represent the energetic connection that you have to each of them. Even though you may hold a great amount of resentment towards the fact that you have held some of the thoughts on your picture, notice that part of you is able to value and appreciate the learning and lesson that each thought has given you.

Right now you are one choice away from a new beginning – one that leads you toward becoming the fullest human being you can be.
Oprah Winfrey

Choose now to love whatever you can, from where you are, in order to let it go. With forgiveness for yourself and for anyone else that comes to mind, connect with a sensation of love within your heart and imagine your diamond shining incredibly brightly and dissolving all of the little energetic cords that once connected you to your thought clutter.

Visualise the thoughts themselves and any remaining attachment you had to them or anything else that you added on your picture being surrounded by love and the brightness of the light from your diamond, as if you are dissolving them in love and brightness. Feel them literally floating away and disintegrating.

When you sense that you have finished dissolving everything around your diamond, take a pair of scissors and cut your diamond out from the piece of paper. This is symbolic of you having chosen to now consciously allow your brilliance to shine.

It is time to recover your energy and rediscover your inner power!

Need-to-Know Summary

- Burnout has become a global cause for concern and an unsustainable framework upon which we are subconsciously building the future of our planet.
- Burnout is not unique to any one sort of personality or profession.
- Burnout is the collective result of various factors cumulating in prolonged stress and poor lifestyle choices that lead to severe depletion of the autoimmune system and adrenal glands.
- Digital overload has contributed to widespread increase of burnout.
- Overwork is entrenched in the culture of many public and private sector organisations.
- Busyness and sleep deprivation have become socially acceptable parts of our collective conditioning because we equate them with status.
- Burnout cannot be blamed entirely on the heavy workloads and expectations that organisations place on their employees.
- Internal drivers combined with external stressors result in burnout; both must be addressed.
- It is possible to learn how to self-regulate by sensing early warning signs before reaching total burnout.
- Symptoms of burnout are experienced emotionally, cognitively, physically, behaviourally, and environmentally.
- Common symptoms include overwhelm, depression, anxiety, headaches, backache, insomnia, constantly feeling tired, dizziness, indigestion problems, inability to relax, and low libido.
- Our bodies communicate with us when things are out of balance.
- By responding to mild physical symptoms, rather than

overriding them, you avoid more serious medical conditions.

- The accumulation of clutter in various life areas is indicative of burnout.
- Lack of self-care results in increased accidents and the breakdown of appliances, cars, and relationships.
- Burnout represents an opportunity for phenomenal personal learning and transformational change.
- Root cause beliefs held since childhood impact the direction of our entire lives.
- By uncovering your thought patterns and conditioning you can shift your mindset and transform your experience from one of *burnout* to one of *brilliance*.

PART 2 – RECOVERY

Recovering Your Energy

The human body consists of billions and billions of tiny atoms, minute pockets of energy all vibrating at various speeds. In fact, everything in the universe consists of variations and combinations of these same atoms of energy, spinning at different frequencies and intensities.

Dr David Hamilton eloquently explains this phenomenon in his book, *Is Your Life Mapped Out?* He believes we are connected to each other and the universe as a whole by our 'chronobiology', the way we (and all other living organisms) synchronise with the movements of the earth, sun and moon.

Some of us are more sensitive to cosmic cycles than others, as is the case for those who suffer with Seasonal Affective Disorder during winter months when there is a shortening of daylight hours and less sunlight. Similarly studies have shown that a significant number of women experience menstruation within 48 hours of the new moon.[27]

Our energy is transmitted by our thoughts and can be picked up by others. In *It's the Thought That Counts*, Dr Hamilton gives examples of how science has demonstrated that we are 'intimately connected to each other in such a way that every thought and feeling sends ripples throughout the entire universe'. Have you ever noticed how just as you are about to say something, someone else says it before you? Or the very moment you are thinking of a friend or relation the phone rings or an email unexpectedly pops in from them?

We each have our own unique energetic vibration that can be intuitively felt by other people, even when we are miles away from each other. The term entrainment is used to describe the phenomena of two or more rhythmical processes synchronising with each other. In the same way that interplanetary forces affect us, the vibrations of other people and places also affect us. Some people and places energise us; others seem to completely zap us of energy.

When we start to notice the people and places that positively benefit our energy versus the ones that drain us, we become empowered to more consciously choose where and with whom we spend our time.

Light Bulb Exercise

I often use the metaphor of a light bulb to help my clients become more aware of how much energy they have available to them, compared to what they feel they are accessing and emanating. Some days you may feel like you are barely capable of being as bright as a night light; other days you may feel you could fill an entire football stadium like a floodlight.

Grab a pen and paper and doodle a picture of a giant light bulb. Do it quickly, this is not a test of your artistic talent!

Now, imagine that this light bulb represents your energy and you are able to gauge the percentage of your own energy supply that you are currently accessing and emitting.

What figure first drops into your head? Write it inside the bulb.

Most people I work with say they feel like a night light, rather than a floodlight, and come up with a figure that is less than 20%.

Miraculously many people, like you, have managed to do some amazing things running on a tiny percentage of the full potential energy supply that they truly have available to them. But, there comes a point where their energy becomes so depleted that they begin to experience diminishing returns in all areas of their life.

What I love about my work is experiencing people shining at their brightest and generating astounding results when they learn how to tap into and sustain the full energy potential that they have available to them to harness.

You can access this too!

Extreme Self-Care

The essential key to recovery from burnout requires developing the art of extreme self-care. This means making a commitment to prioritise your own health and wellbeing above all else.

If you struggle with the concept of putting yourself before others, think about the emergency procedure announcement routinely made on airplanes instructing you to stay calm and make sure that you securely fasten your own oxygen mask *before* helping anyone else.

You are of no use to anyone unless you first take care of yourself.

Often when I ask a client to tell me about the last time they did something by themselves, for themselves, there will be a long pause. The response, after a while spent thinking about the question, is usually 'I can't remember'.

When we give ourselves permission to have some 'me time' and get away from it all, we return with far more energy and enthusiasm to share with others. When given space to think we often have breakthrough ideas that result in us being able to return to our work or family life and implement all kinds of solutions to problems that we otherwise would have struggled to overcome.

How often have you noticed that some of your best ideas and insights arrive while you are in the shower, taking a morning run, meditating, walking or even sleeping?

Says Jessica Herrin, CEO of Stella and Dot:

My morning run is when my head is most clear and when I synthesize all of the things that are going on in my head. When I'm running I'm always three to five years out in my mind. As a leader that's where I need to spend time.

Sometimes we simply need a creative 'jump start' to come up with a way of carving out the thinking space that we need. For example, Thomas Edison would take an hour out almost every day and trundle off with his fishing rod to sit alone at the dock and fish. People respected this part of his daily routine because they accepted the fact that he loved to fish. They were, however, curious, when he always returned with an empty basket, how someone so keen on fishing could be so very bad at it.

The truth was that Edison never caught any fish because he never used any bait. Because it was his fishing time, his staff didn't disturb him. And because he used no bait, the fish didn't disturb him either. He created the perfect thinking space allowing him time for vision and re-evaluation, powerful moments to generate genius ideas.

In order to avoid, recover from or prevent a burnout, it is imperative to regularly ensure you take time out for yourself.

Actor and yoga teacher Samantha Cullen learned the value of solitude one year when she found herself 'depleted, overworked, lonely, and far from home'. As a single woman living on her own she says she often used to feel the need to fill her time and as a result would overschedule her life. To help her overcome this habit she challenged herself to take a weekend out and not plan anything.

I didn't make any dates, schedule any appointments, or find more work to do. Instead, I spent the weekend with myself. I drove to the coast and back, made home-cooked meals, read, practiced yoga, and took myself out for ice cream and long walks through the city. It felt uncomfortable at first, but it was the beginning of learning how to live with myself.

Since then, the more I choose solitude (when needed), by saying no to others and yes to myself, the more comfortable and nurtured I feel. A wise friend told me how she differentiated solitude from isolation. Isolation, she said, is cutting yourself off from others, while solitude is making friends with yourself so that you can foster your relationship with others. I often picture myself as a battery that sometimes runs low and needs to recharge – and the recharging is most efficient when I'm alone.

Some signals that tell me I need to recharge are irritability, the inability to concentrate or listen well, not being present with people, lack of compassion, and judgment toward others and myself. I come back to the visual image of plugging myself into a socket in order to refuel.

We all need this kind of relaxation time and thinking space to recharge our batteries and unleash our creative genius. How can you create yours? Experiment with it today.

Get your diary or calendar on your computer and commit to scheduling 20 minutes of 'me' time for yourself each day and one whole extra hour each week – minimum.

Write or type it in.

No excuses.

I know! At the suggestion of this, your inner slave driver is wildly protesting about how that just isn't possible for you for numerous reasons that will seem like valid excuses for yet again shelving your own needs. Stand up to her.

You can find a way to do this. In fact, you *have* to. Your recovery depends upon it.

Imagine what it would feel like to be trapped on the burnout treadmill, much the same as if you were on a runner's treadmill that wouldn't switch off?

Consider it for a moment.

What would be the benefits for you if you put this book down right now, ignored any insight you have gained and chose not to change anything in your life?

It would be easier not to change. But, what would the cost be?

How might your health, relationships, career, finances and love life suffer a few months or years from now if you kept struggling on?

When Carrie Kerpen became CEO of Likeable Media, she had

been burning herself out under the pressure of running a rapidly-growing business, parenting her two children and caring for her dying father. Exercise and healthy eating had long gone out of the window, and she had been surviving on leftover mac and cheese from her five-year-old daughter's plate or client lunches that always included a giant dessert. Carrie was tipping the scales at 223 pounds.

She urgently identified self-care as the most critical step she needed to take in order to become the face of the organisation and 'make sure the management team was top notch'. In order for Carrie to be a great leader she realised that she had to first focus on herself.

It's funny, people say that you can't get healthy until you're really ready. Nothing motivated me. Not losing my dad to cancer. Not wearing plus-size clothing. Not feeling less attractive. What motivated me finally was stepping into the CEO role at Likeable Media.

I realized that to be a great leader, I had to focus on myself... I needed to be fit-both mentally and physically.

The first thing I did was set goals. In my first quarter as CEO, the first three months of 2013, I wanted to lose 20 percent of my body weight. I also wanted to eliminate processed foods, cook dinner three nights a week for my family, and take a class in something – anything, really – that interested me.

I met with a nutritionist weekly – which was tough to do with my crazy calendar, but I made it a priority.

I started a gratitude journal. Every day, I wrote three things that I was grateful for. When something amazing happened in a meeting, I would stop and write it down. If I didn't have the journal on me, I would hop out of the meeting and grab it.

I gave up coffee, and I started making juices. My staff did not understand how their once Dunkin Donuts-obsessed leader was now drinking kale smoothies. They made fun of my 'vomit juice' –

and I laughed along with them – but it didn't stop me.

I took up spinning and Zumba, and I even took an online course in business finance – something I've been passionate about and learned along the way but was never formally trained in.

And, most importantly, three days a week, I took the 4:47 train home, and I cooked dinner for my family.

My staff was a bit confused, but supportive. And that quarter, I lost 20 percent of my body weight, eliminated most processed foods, took a class or two – and built the life that I wanted.

I saw results at work

And then, it became easier to meet my goals at work. In fact, I didn't just meet them. I crushed them. I became more focused, more present and more confident. My employees, inspired by what I was doing, started to focus on their own personal goals. This makes them better at what they do, too.

Balance Wheel Exercise

Grab a pen and use the diagram below to help you take stock on how you currently feel about the various areas of your life and what the impact on these areas would be further down the line if you kept repeating the same burnout patterns in your life.

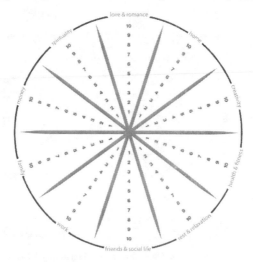

Assess each area of your life by using the balance wheel to help give a score to your level of satisfaction on 0 (low) to 10 (high). Circle your scores.

Join the scores you have circled around the wheel.

Ask yourself the following questions:

1. What first strikes you as you look at your wheel?
2. What else do you notice?
3. What area(s) has greatest impact?
4. What area(s) is a priority to change?
5. Is anything missing? Would you add a segment?
6. How would things be different if that segment were at the right level?
7. How would you sum up your wheel?
8. What really needs to change?
9. What would you be feeling, seeing, hearing if that area changed?
10. What impact would making that change have on each area of your life?

If you are committed to making that change, then read on!

Change Your Lifestyle Habits

If you have been running on reserves for a while it is likely that your exercise, diet and sleep routines have suffered as a result.

Now is the time to rebalance them.

How healthy are your daily lifestyle habits?

I previously mentioned the impact of cumulative stress on the adrenal system. When recovering from burnout it is important to help the adrenal glands recuperate slowly and steadily.

Resume exercise gently and gradually; otherwise you could do more harm than good. Speak to your doctor about a graduated program. Ease yourself into things and listen to your body.

You Are What You Eat

Below are some general guidelines for what to eat in order to help replenish exhausted adrenals.

I additionally advise you to consult a nutritionist who can specifically advise you on how best to rebuild your immune system based on your height, weight, sex, body type and medical history. For optimal wellness, also speak with your local health food store about dietary supplements from which you might benefit.

- Aim for a varied diet of whole natural foods.
- Buy organic wherever possible.
- Drink a glass of water with a squeeze of fresh lemon at breakfast when you wake in the morning.
- Eat breakfast within one hour of starting your day.
- Combine a source of protein, healthy fat and whole grains (as a source of carbohydrate) with every meal.
- When using oil for cooking or dressings, opt for cold-pressed olive, flax, grapeseed or safflower.
- Increase your general consumption of green leafy vegetables to help boost your intake of vitamins, minerals and phytonutrients.
- Include seaweed and other sea vegetables in your diet where possible. (They have been found to contain virtually all of the nutrients that are found in the ocean in addition to many of the same minerals found in human blood.)

Overcoming Sleep Deprivation

I learned the hard way the value of sleep. Three and a half years ago I fainted from exhaustion. I hit my head on my desk. I broke my cheekbone. I got five stitches in my right eye. And I began a journey of rediscovering the value of sleep. And in the course of that, I studied, I met with medical doctors and scientists…. the way to a

more productive, more inspired, more joyful life... is getting enough sleep.
Arianna Huffington, CEO Huffington Post

In many corporate cultures admitting the need for sleep is like showing a sign of weakness. Many men and women brag about their lack of sleep as if it were something to be proud of.

Sleep is one of the most important things our bodies need yet often is what we cut out first when we are burning the candle at both ends. It is not just because of sleep deprivation one-upmanship that many people are not getting the rest that they need. When our to-do lists seem never-ending we can be easily tempted to stay up late in order to get through everything rather than reexamining our priorities and looking at what we can drop from the list.

The effect of skimping on sleep for prolonged periods of time puts your health at serious risk. A study conducted by the University of Surrey in the UK[28] discovered that just one week of insufficient sleep 'alters the gene expression in human blood cells, reduces the amplitude of circadian rhythms in gene expression, and intensifies the effects of subsequent acute total sleep loss on gene expression'. The effects of this can cause more than 700 genetic changes contributing to severe negative health outcomes including obesity, cardiovascular disease and cognitive impairment.

Sleep is critical to rebuilding the body and maintaining a functional state, all kinds of damage appear to occur. If we can't actually replenish and replace new cells, then that's going to lead to degenerative diseases.
Colin Smith, PhD, University of Surrey

In a nutshell, it is incredibly important to ensure that you get as much sleep as you need. According to the National Sleep

Foundation, most adults require a minimum of seven to nine hours good quality sleep per night.

If you have been experiencing difficulty sleeping refer back to the *Insomnia* section on page 32 in addition to checking out the *Get Enough Sleep Section* on page 226.

If you have been fighting fatigue with an illness like post viral fatigue syndrome, chronic fatigue, ME or similar then you may feel that you have slept enough to last a lifetime. The problem is that your body is likely to keep you stuck in the experience of fatigue until it trusts your mind to listen when it needs rest *and* to prioritise self-care by following strategies for sustainable success. Part 3 of this book will help you to break free from fatigue by creating your own map, vision and strategies for the future.

Remember, you cannot fix a problem with the same mindset that created it. You need to find a new approach in order to design and build the life you truly desire to live.

Learn to Say 'No'

In order to prioritise sufficient self-care in the form of rest, relaxation, sleep, exercise, healthy food and other lifestyle choices, it is necessary to create time and space for these things in your life.

Time is the most valuable asset that you have.

It is important to honour and protect it. In order to do this effectively you need to learn how to say 'no'.

I previously introduced the concept of time clutter. Clearing your time clutter is like clearing your closet, only instead of throwing out old clothes, you let go of expired commitments, and instead of buying more shoes, you learn to say no to taking on extra things.

Saying 'no' can present a real challenge. Many people find it hard to say no for fear of disappointing others. When we agree to something simply to keep someone else happy or to avoid letting him or her down, we betray our own needs.

Do you find yourself getting roped into commitments,

projects or even romantic dates that you have no interest in?

Are you letting people walk all over you because you're unable to express how you really feel?

Have you been passed over for promotions and ignored in meetings when you need to be heard?

If you find yourself saying 'yes', when you really mean 'no', or 'not now', try pausing for a moment the next time someone asks you to do something for him or her. Instead of instantly responding with 'yes' and over committing yourself to doing too much, buy yourself some time to think about your response by answering the question with another question.

Respond positively with 'I'd like to help you AND right now I need to do XXX. Can you come back to me later if you still need me?'

By doing this you position yourself as being prepared to help but set a boundary for the other person to respect that you are already busy. You also sow the seed that the person might not need you later because by then they might just have solved their issue without you.

For some people, just hearing you say 'no', regardless of how you frame it, will challenge their relationship with you. This is because by saying 'no' to them when they are used to automatically hearing 'yes' you change the status quo regarding the expectations they place on you. Instead of feeling guilty and attempting to over-explain, excuse, defend or argue about how you feel, stay strong and keep things concise.

Lovingly assert yourself.

You teach people how to treat you. Your behaviours become habits, and people learn to expect the same thing from you regardless of the situation.

Two different people in the same job could be treated very differently depending on how they each conduct themselves, the boundaries they set and the results they routinely obtain.

It is never too late to set new boundaries for yourself in any area of your life.

Commitment Clearing

How enthusiastic do you feel about the commitments you have in your life?

Do they fuel your energy or deplete you?

Every time we accept a request from someone else we are investing our energy in something that will inspire and ignite us, or we are sacrificing the opportunity to be doing something else with our time.

When our days become filled with commitments that we resent this can eat away at us and exhaust our energy and enthusiasm.

Yahoo CEO Marissa Mayer has an interesting theory that burnout is strongly linked to resentment. She says you can beat burnout by knowing what it is you are giving up that makes you resentful:

I tell people: find your rhythm. Your rhythm is what matters to you so much that when you miss it you're resentful of your work. I had a young guy, just out of college, and I saw some early burnout signs. I said, "Think about it and tell me what your rhythm is." He came back and said, "Tuesday night dinners. My friends from college, we all get together every Tuesday night and do a potluck. If I miss it, the whole rest of the week I'm like, 'I'm just not going to stay late tonight. I didn't even get to do my Tuesday night dinner.'" So now we know that Nathan can never miss Tuesday night dinner again. It's just that simple. You're going to be so much more productive the rest of the week if you get that.

Imagine if every day of your life was spent only doing the things that you *really* wanted to do.

How much more energy would you have?

Commitment Exercise

Reflect on each area of your life and use Table 2.1 (found at the end of this chapter) to help you list each of your commitments.

Once you have written your commitments down do a quick check on each one to identify how enthusiastic you feel about each one. Ask yourself: 'On a scale of 0 -10, how enthusiastic do I feel about this?'

After rating each commitment, take a look at the ones with the lowest scores. If you were no longer involved with these things what difference would that make to your life?

Could letting them go create the space you need for self-care? And if clearing them gave you plenty of time to look after yourself, what might be some of the other more exciting things you could focus on in their place?

Mind Map Exercise

With your focus on the positive impact that clearing old commitments would have in your life, create a mind map or thought shower diagram to help you explore the action steps you would need to take in order to withdraw your time and energy.

Useful Phrases

To become a pro at saying 'no', practice some responses to likely scenarios in front of a mirror with your coach or a supportive friend.

Here are some examples of tactful ways to truthfully decline future demands on your time and energy. While they have a friendly and respectful tone, they are purposefully short and direct to help you avoid over-explaining. Tailor them to fit the kind of requests you routinely receive:

'Thank you for your invitation/request to xxx; I am honored that you thought to ask me. While I am unable to accept/partic-ipate/commit to this right now, I wish you every success with the event/project'.

'In order to keep other commitments I have made, I am unable to participate with xxx at the moment. If circumstances change then I will be sure to let you know'.

'I'm sorry to disappoint you, but I am unable to get involved with xxx at this time. Let me know if you need some help coming up with an alternative solution'.

Zero Toleration

It is likely not only that old commitments in your life have been draining your energy but also negative people and places.

My guess if you are feeling burnt out is that you are spending more time with what I refer to as 'energy vampires', rather than 'energy radiators'. You are likely also to be spending more time in places that deplete your energy rather than refueling it.

We all tolerate certain things in life, but did you know that the very things you are tolerating are likely to be holding you back from experiencing the ultimate success you so desperately want to experience?

By tolerating certain people, places and situations we place boulders before our brilliance, often in an unconscious attempt to protect ourselves from the risk of failure or paradoxically from the risk of shining too brightly.

Our deepest fear is not that we are inadequate. Our deepest fear is that we are powerful beyond measure. It is our light, not our darkness that most frightens us.
Marianne Williamson

Whenever we get stuck in negative thinking and behaviour that keeps us small, unseen, and *saving* rather than *serving*, we stay in the shadow of our fears and uncertainties and prevent ourselves from experiencing our true power, following our passions and fulfilling our purpose.

An easy way to identify areas where you are tolerating is by noticing whenever your energy feels drained and whenever you choose thoughts or behaviours that correspond with beliefs of worthlessness, self-sacrificing and suffering, all of which are unhealthy to your well-being.

As you bring this into your awareness notice whether any part of you wants to place blame on others or on your circumstances, thus externalising any responsibility. Blaming is unproductive and energetically draining. Instead, accept that what has happened has happened so that you can release resentment. Blame-based thoughts include:

'Why me?'
'What have I done to deserve this?'
'If only he hadn't xxx.'
'If only she didn't xxx.'
'It's all because of them.'
'It's his/her/their/my fault.'
'I have everyone's troubles on my shoulders.'
'Other people dump stuff on me.'
'Other people exhaust me.'
'He/she/it's a pain in the neck.'

You can reclaim your power by deciding to view the things you tolerate in your life from a different vantage point, looking instead for the learning opportunity that they present. There is a fear-based belief buried behind each toleration, which is attempting to keep you safe, small and protected from your true, expanded and enlightened magnificence.

If you explore it deeply enough you can uncover the lesson for you to learn, the pain for you to heal, the person you need to forgive or the belief you need to release in order to overcome your fear, let go, move forward, embrace your true power and potential and start choosing what you were truly born to experience in your life.

If you don't take notice and restore the situation, the same thing or similar will keep happening.
Olive Hickmott

Cyclical patterns of self-destruction can keep us stuck by replaying similar eventualities and relationships. When we explore what we are truly tolerating in our beliefs about ourselves, leading to our decisions and ultimately our behaviours, then we give ourselves back the opportunity to choose to release anything past its due date and shift into our greatness. Once we acknowledge, resolve and let them go, we are able to move on quickly to opportunities aligned with our highest good and unleash our unlimited potential.

Blame and Toleration Exercise

Here are five simple steps to help you let go of blame and toleration:

1. **Create a list** of all the things, people, or situations that you feel you have been tolerating.

2. **Identify the core beliefs** you have been holding that have led to each toleration, e.g.,:

    'I am not worth x.'
    'I must be x.'
    'I am scared of x.'
    'It is my duty to x.'
    'I should/ought to x.'

3. **Release the energy** of these negative beliefs by burning the paper you have written them on.[29]

4. **Create positive affirmations** to replace your old beliefs.

An affirmation is a statement you make in the present tense, to yourself, to counteract a negative belief. For example, instead of entertaining the thought 'I can't do this', chose instead to affirm 'I can do this, and I can do it now!'

5. **Release old memories with forgiveness** so you can move on. If you have been holding resentment or anger from painful past experiences it is important to find a way to let go and release any fantasy that the past could somehow have played out differently.

Forgiveness

Sometimes it can be difficult to forgive other people because it can feel like you are condoning their actions. But forgiveness is not about agreeing with wrongdoings; rather it is about finding a place in your heart to acknowledge that whatever someone did that was emotionally, psychologically or physically hurtful to you was not a true reflection of who they really are but instead a mistake they made about how to conduct themselves.

Your mind is like a video recorder. Every little detail of your life has been recorded and stored in your mind. Some memories are much easier to recall than others. The powerful thing about our mind is that we can use our imagination to change the feelings we hold in relation to our memories and release any associated hurt or pain by giving our memories alternative endings.

You can try this now.

Forgiveness Exercise

Bring to mind a memory that you would like to move on from. Replay the event in your mind's eye as if you were watching it on a television screen rather than re-experiencing it energetically. Observe what took place, who said what to whom and how you responded.

What happened at that time that made the experience a problem for you?

Knowing that you did the best you could at the time given the thoughts you were thinking and the knowledge you then had available to you, forgive yourself for any resentment you have held about not having conducted yourself differently in any way. Imagine you are opening your heart and sending love from the 'you' in the current moment, here and now, to the 'you' back then. Visualise that sensation of love dissolving any bitterness or self-loathing.

Imagine completely surrounding your past self with love, comfort and support.

Next, extend that sensation of love and forgiveness to anyone else involved in the memory. Again, visualise that sensation of love dissolving any anger or ill feeling. You are not condoning actions but forgiving the choice made at the time.

Walking Away

In a similar way to clearing your calendar of commitments we are now going to explore how you can actively distance yourself from people or places that drain you.

Taking steps toward doing this is likely to bring up familiar feelings of guilt about letting people down or fear about what people will think. But every small change you make has a big impact on the trajectory of your future.

Envisage being an astronaut in a space rocket heading for a black hole (aka burnout). Now imagine heading toward a beautiful planet named 'Brilliance' instead. Each positive mindset shift you make steers you away from the black hole and aligns your rocket with brilliance.

You are worth anything it takes to stay bound for Brilliance. You cannot serve anyone when you are in a place of exhaustion. If you feel that a particular environment, person or group of people is depleting your energy or diminishing your inner power then it is vital that you address how you can change this. The key is to learn how to protect, maintain and manage your energy.

Energy Management

The importance of restoration is rooted in our physiology... Human beings aren't designed to expend energy continuously. Rather, we're meant to pulse between spending and recovering energy.
Tony Schwartz

I was first introduced to the concept of energy management when I began practicing martial arts. At the core of martial arts philosophy lies ancient energy management principles that can be used to help prevent and overcome burnout by bringing body, mind and spirit into balance.

As a child my father used to teach me techniques from the Japanese martial arts of judo, karate and ju-jitsu. When I was twelve years old I joined an Ishinryu style karate club and trained under Peter Dennis 8th Dan, who taught me a powerful combination of Wado-Ryu, Kyokushinkai and Shotokan techniques, encompassing a head, heart, body and mind philosophy. I achieved my black belt in karate in 1997 and was recognised by BUCS (British Universities & Colleges Sport) as an elite sportswoman studying at the University of Surrey.

There were no karate clubs in the Guildford area offering training to the international standard that I had received from Sensei Dennis, so I explored other martial arts. I discovered an excellent taekwondo club run by Master Nyeong Woo Nam from Korea, where I was able to continue training at an advanced level. During my time at university I trained with taekwondo, karate and kickboxing clubs in Germany, Spain and the USA. I became a certified *KickBoxFitness* Instructor in 2000 and was awarded a black belt in taekwondo in 2002.

Master Nam taught me how taekwondo philosophy represents changes and movements in human beings through the separate elements of 'Eum' (Negative or Darkness), 'Yang' (Positive or Light), 'Cheon' (Heaven), 'Ji' (Earth), and 'In' (Man) – which are all one and the same. This serves as a powerful metaphor for life: by allowing flow and internal state change within ourselves, we can continuously change skills and never get stuck, in any situation.

When I was recovering from burnout I drew on these principles to help me change the negative thought patterns that had been keeping me stuck. I also used my martial arts training to help me restore, recharge and protect my energy.

In the Western world, people are often attracted to martial arts as a way of learning how to protect themselves physically. Physical defense skills are only one element of martial arts teachings. The way of the warrior is also about harmonising mind, body and soul, as well as mastering how to harness and protect the infinite power within.

One of the first things I learned as a karate student was how to avoid and prevent an attack. Defence against any negative situation begins first with energetic protection.

Energetic self-defence is equally as important as physical self-defence.

Our personal energy is assaulted on an almost continuous basis as we move through our modern lives. We are attacked every time we tune in to negative news announcements, take part in gossip, spend time in places or with people who drain us, and participate in activities we dislike. Energy protection techniques can help us minimise the weakening effect of external influences on our energy.

There are many different approaches to energy protection around the world. Some are long and complex involving rituals and ceremonies, others simple and quick. Such techniques are engrained in many cultures of the world yet still remain largely unknown to others.

The technique I most regularly teach and practice myself is very powerful yet also extremely easy. All that it requires is for you to turn your attention inwards and set an intention to shield yourself from the effects of anything or anyone that may negatively influence your energy.

Protection Process

Either follow these simple steps by reading through the directions outlined below or listen to the audio recording of this protection process as a mini guided meditation, which you will find on the webpage for this book: www.jaynemorris.com.

1. **Turn your focus to your breath.** Take a deep breath inward; relax your body and mind. Close your eyes if you wish.

2. **Notice any tension** you are holding in your body; if there is a feeling of tightness, contraction, stress or fatigue being held anywhere in your body, acknowledge it and imagine the tension easing away with each breath you take, gently releasing, like melting butter. With each out breath let go of anything worrying you.

3. **Observe your thoughts** as if they are clouds floating into your consciousness; just as gently as they float in, allow them to float past again, trusting that you can let go of them for now and come back to them anytime you like later.

4. **Place your attention inside** and sense the core of your being, your energy centre, just below your rib cage. You may sense this as a ball of light, or sense it as a precious gem or stone, or you may sense your energy centre as a different shape. Notice its colour and size.

5. **Take ownership** of the energy at the core of your being.

It holds all you ever have been and all your possibilities for the future. With your next breath imagine the energy from the centre of your being radiating across your entire body.

6. **Imagine yourself inside a big zorbing ball,** sending that energy outwards from your core, in every direction possible, filling the entire area around you with your inner light and power.

7. **Visualise replenishing and recharging** every cell in your body with this energy from within. Feel yourself positively glowing. This energy is your true power, your true self – it is infinite and boundless.

8. **Envisage surrounding your zorbing ball with a layer of protection.** Make this layer any colour and texture that you choose. Visualise it being completely impenetrable by any negative external energies.

9. **Affirm to yourself** that only positive energy of love and peace can pass through this special layer of protection.

10. **Bring your awareness back** to the present moment with your next breath knowing that you are now protected for the rest of the day/evening ahead.

The more often you take yourself through this process the quicker you will get at it. With practice you will soon find that you can use it anytime and anywhere to help clear your energy and keep it protected.

Maria Zoutsou has been using this technique at the start of each day since completing a VIP day with me, she says:

Not only do I see a change in my energy, others have noticed it too. My daughter in Greece has commented on how different I sound and my new positive outlook on things. She even said, "Mum, you are the happiest I've ever seen you! What's changed?"

Since my VIP day I have experienced big changes in my relation-ships with others and in my approach to my career too. Things in all areas seem to be unfolding effortlessly. In fact, I feel there is an element of surprise in my new endeavors, and somehow I feel I will be pleasantly surprised by their results!

Exhausting Statements

Our energy follows our thoughts, and the phrases we repeat to ourselves as part of our internal dialogue, in addition to what we say out loud in conversations with others, become our reality.

In order to improve the results we experience in any area of our lives we need to improve our thinking. The Empowerment Cycle[30] below shows the knock-on effect that our thoughts have on our language, action, habits and ultimately, our results.

Empowerment Cycle

It is time to release any of the thoughts that have been draining your energy and impacting your language, action, habits and results so that you can replace them with energy-affirming ones.

Common statements that my clients routinely identify as having the biggest impact on their energy include the following:

'I am always so busy.'

'I am rushed off my feet.'

'I am shattered.'

'I am like a yo-yo.'

'I am all over the place.'

'I am here, there, and everywhere.'

'I am knocked out.'

'I am always struggling.'

'I am always on the go.'

'I am helpless.'

'All my fuses are blown.'

'I am like a zombie.'

'I am sick and tired of xxx.'

'XXX makes me sick to the stomach.'

'I have no energy.'

These phrases typically result in the continued experience of exhaustion and manifest themselves metaphorically as various illnesses.

Energy Magnet Exercise

You can let go of the draining effect of these metaphors by following this simple energy management exercise.

Stand with your feet shoulder-width apart and your palms facing outwards from your body. Take three deep breaths. Bring to mind any of the phrases that you have identified with that have been contributing to your exhaustion.

Imagine there is a large magnet above your head and another one beneath your feet. These magnets can be any colour you choose, and you control the strength of them. Allow them to draw out any negative energy that has been clogging up your energy system. Release anything that has been draining you, holding you back or making you feel tired and heavy, as if they are being lifted from you by these powerful magnets.

Whenever you sense that they have pulled away everything

that you need them to, you can switch them off, and they will automatically transmute all the negative energy they are now holding into positive healing energy. In your mind's eye you may notice that the magnets change colour as they do this.

When you sense that all the negative energy has changed into positive energy you can switch the magnets back on again, and this time they will send you a gentle flow of positive energy to help recharge and re-energise you. Imagine this positive energy flowing through all of the cells in your body, healing and replenishing them.

When you sense that the process is complete take three deep breaths and bring your awareness back to the present moment.

Should, Must, Ought

There are three words that instantly move us out of the positive energy of *flow* and into a negative energy of *forcing*. These are 'should', 'must' or 'ought'.

We sometimes use these words in relation to actions we feel resistance towards taking and can also place them both verbally or non-verbally as judgements or demands upon other people, for example, 'Fred should support me'.

In *The Work,* Byron Katie suggests that rather than suppressing these kind of 'should, must or ought' judgements that we hold about others, we can use them as starting points for self-realisation. What we see in other people is a mirror of what we have not yet realised about ourselves. You can use her turn-around framework to help you explore and release the negative energy of such statements by following these examples to help you unravel and release your own:

'He should support me' turns around to:

- He shouldn't support me. (This is reality.)
- I should support him.

- I should support myself.

And, to take things one step further, finally replace the 'should' with a positive, affirming, and energising new statement, e.g.,:

- I am always supported.
- Support comes to me in miraculous ways.
- Life supports me.

Positive affirmations are a powerful tool to help reprogramme your thinking. We have as humans the unique capacity to evolve our thoughts and actions. By changing our thinking we literally reshape our brain and our destiny. Every thought we hold and how we consciously or unconsciously fabricate each affirms our neurological sense of self, so whatever you spend your time mentally attending to, that is who you are and what you will become.

Dr Joe Dispenza explains that the reason we cling to relationships or jobs that drive us to experience 'confusion, unhappiness, aggression, and even depression' is that we can become addicted to the stress chemicals that are aroused when we get stuck in a negative mindset and attitude. To break free from this we need to evolve our brain by using its 'natural capacity of neuroplasticity – the ability to rewire and create new neural circuits at any age – to make substantial changes'.

The way that we can do this is to simply pay attention to our thoughts, notice whether they are aligned with a positive outcome, and if they are not conducive to what we want, then change them so that they reflect the true reality of that which we desire to experience.

This is empowering because it creates new neurological pathways for our thinking to follow. Without doing this we would instead revert automatically to old conditioned thinking and associated negative memories, feelings and emotions from our past.

The brain does not know the difference between what it is thinking (internal) and what it experiences (external). So by visualising what we most want to experience in the future, ahead of the potential event or outcome actually taking place, we access the possible positive feelings available to us in the present moment and imprint them in our memory. This then enables us to create new, positive and inspiring experiences in our lives because our brains begin to generate thoughts aligned with our positive intentions and visualisations for the future instead of re-running old programming from our past.

Begin to notice the little voice in your head and observe the thoughts you have in relation to your goals so that you can replace non-supportive beliefs with a more supportive way of thinking.

Taking any action because you feel we 'should, must or ought to' means you override your intuitive guidance. Whenever you notice this happening, try to pause for a moment and ask yourself: 'What next course of action would be for my highest good?' Trust your first response, without judging. Give yourself permission to follow whatever you feel like doing next – you may surprise yourself with what you come up with. Amazing results are sure to follow!

Energy Maintenance

We are often so generous, especially with ourselves, that we give little pieces of ourselves away, to almost anyone who asks. At the time, we hardly notice. Sometimes the pieces we give away are so minuscule that they really seem unimportant… we are unaware of the cumulative effect of years of giving away little bits and pieces of ourselves… Giving myself away and being stingy are not my only options. I can share myself and not give myself away.
Anne Wilson Shaef

Energy protection can help us give to other people without being drained by them. Sometimes, however, we need to completely disconnect from people and commitments in our lives that have been excessively depleting us or no longer inspire us.

Depending on the circumstances, you may feel you need to completely cut certain people out of your life, quit your job or move house. Trust your gut if you have an overwhelming feeling that you need to totally disconnect in order to move forward. The following questions may help you to hear your inner voice of wisdom. In each instance take action aligned with the answer that your heart gives you in response:

Relationship
'If I knew this person would not be angry or upset with me, would I let them go from my life?'

Home
'If I knew that by leaving this home xxx (insert perceived fear) would not be a problem for me, would I still want to move?'

Job
'If I knew that xxx (insert perceived fear) was not an issue, would I want to quit my role as xxx?'

Where your answer to any of the questions above is a resounding 'yes' then follow the next exercise to help you disconnect energetically from the person, place or situation. This will help you to stay calm and gain clarity on the next best course of action to take.

It takes courage to begin something, but it can take even more to end it.
Marie Forleo

Be bold. You can clear the way for a new future path.

Energetically Disconnecting

Everything on the planet is energy of some form or another. As I mentioned in *Learning from Your Past* we are comprised of countless energetic sources and components. Water plays an important part in managing our energy because water molecules absorb energy, and the average human body is 50-75% comprised of water.

Dr Masaru Emoto, a Japanese author and entrepreneur[31] conducted years of research, strenuously observing crystals of water from various sources. Emoto studied the effect of exposing water of varying qualities to the energetic vibration of different words, pictures and music, then freezing them. He then examined the resulting crystals with microscopic photography and observed fascinating results:

We always observed beautiful crystals after giving good words, playing good music, and showing, playing or offering pure prayer to water. On the other hand, we observed disfigured crystals in the opposite situation.

Emoto found that pristine water from preserved natural rivers and lakes produced stunning crystal formations whereas tap water and water from rivers or lakes near big cities produced distorted and fragmented crystals when frozen. If, however, the water from non-pristine sources was exposed to the energy of positive words, music, pictures or prayer, beautiful crystals formed when frozen.

Based on this research Emoto formed the hypothesis that the human consciousness has an effect on the molecular structure of water. This means that our thoughts, intentions and emotions, both positive and negative, have the power to change our energetic vibration, as do those of others.

The core of our energy is often called our life force energy. Several psychological, philosophical and spiritual theorists refer to this energy as *physis*, meaning the self's natural universal energy.[32] Our life force energy emanates all around us, creating what is referred to as our energy field or aura.

The texts and teachings of tantric and yogic traditions of Hinduism and Buddhism present the concept of *chakras* within the energy field. Chakra is an ancient Sanskrit word, which literally means 'spinning wheel of energy'. These wheels are smaller energy centres within the aura. There are seven key chakras, which are each connected to and associated with a different part of the physical body.[33]

The chakras receive, transmit and assimilate all energy coming into, flowing through and going out of the body. They also help to distribute energy for our physical, emotional, mental and spiritual functions. When our chakras are balanced and clear we are physically healthy and vital, have plenty of energy and are very intuitive.

Due to the increasing popularity of practices such as yoga and meditation, the concept of chakras is becoming more widely accepted, understood and integrated into mainstream Western culture. If this brief introduction has prompted you to explore further, I would recommend reading one of the many books that have been written on this topic.

Psychologists believe that we have an intrinsic natural aspiration for 'growth and development towards health' (Clarkson, 1992)[34]; however the healthy flow of our energy can become disrupted or blocked due to stress, fear, worries and anxieties, in addition to emotions of grief, guilt, disgust, intolerance, sadness, impatience, restlessness, indecisiveness, hurt, regret, jealousy, anger and rage.

Other people and places can also interrupt our energy flow. In the same way that energy naturally flows around our body, it also gets passed from person to person and from person to environment and vice versa. This is why being around positive people and in positive places energises us, whereas negative people and places deplete us.

Swiss psychiatrist and psychotherapist Carl Jung[35], who founded analytical psychology proposed the concept of the collective unconscious:

Our personal psychology is just a thin skin, a ripple on the ocean of collective psychology. The powerful factor, the factor which changes our whole life, which changes the surface of our known world, which makes history, is collective psychology, which moves according to laws entirely different from those of our [individual] consciousness.

We are all energetically connected, like individual strands of a giant spider's web. Every interaction that we have with a person or place strengthens the energetic connections between us. These connections are strongest between the people and places that have played a significant role in our lives, for example our parents or caregivers, siblings, partners, teachers, employers, close friends, homes and places of work.

We're not just little hunks of meat. We're vibrating like a tuning fork — we send out a vibration to other people. We broadcast and receive. Thus the emotions orchestrate the interactions among all our organs and systems to control that.
Dr Candace Pert

Energetic connections between places and people towards which we hold a great amount of love, mutual respect, gratitude and appreciation are very beneficial to our emotional, physical, psychological, and spiritual health and well-being. However any energy stemming from negative emotions is also passed between us and has a detrimental effect on our energy system.

People and places both from our past and present can drain

us. Even when a relationship with someone has ended, we have moved home or changed jobs, we can still feel energetically exhausted if we have not cleared residual electro-magnetic energy attachments.

These energy-based attachments keep old history alive, inwardly repeating events or energies that you would just as soon forget.
Rose Rosetree

Negative energy attachments form very easily as a result of any fearful or negative thinking, even if it is subconscious. Negative language signals causing fear-based attachments include:

- Internal Commands (refer to list presented in *Your Burnout Script* on page 44).
- Judgment – including beliefs (whether spoken or unspoken) that others should behave or not behave in a certain way according to our own judgment of what they 'should/ought to/must be or do'.
- Internalised limiting beliefs in relation to how we feel we personally 'should/ought to/must' behave in response to someone else. These beliefs will feel forced, incongruent and out of alignment with how we truly desire to react.
- Projections – unconsciously rejecting one's own unacceptable attributes by ascribing them to other people.[36]
- Guilt, blame, or shame.

Negative beliefs are also formed at any stage when we participate in psychological 'games' with another person. One common type of game occurs whenever someone draws another person (or more) into a dysfunctional interchange, commonly referred to as 'triangulation', by assuming the role of either:

Victim – thereby holding the belief 'I'm blameless' and wanting to feel safe by experiencing unconditional love from someone else. One may outwardly give the appearance of trying hard to resolve a situation but will have an unconscious hidden motive not to succeed, or to succeed in a way that only benefits the one.

Persecutor – thereby holding the belief 'I'm Right' and adopting a stance of false power by pressurising, coercing or persecuting someone else (the victim).

Rescuer – thereby holding the belief 'I'm good' and falsely believing one will be accepted by others if he or she seemingly intervenes out of a desire to help the situation or the victim.

Whenever this form of psychological interchange occurs players will often move around the triangle, changing roles and suffering the situation until their unconscious psychological needs are met. The series of transactions that ensue as part of such a 'game' create negative attachments between the players because they represent inauthentic substitution for more genuine emotional interaction. This kind of game can be avoided by consciously choosing to step outside the triangle and observe, rather than participate, in such habitual negative behaviour.

The cumulative effect of negative attachments and the endurance of such energy consuming psychological games contribute towards burnout. I have found that it is common for those working in caregiving, teaching, and public-protection professions, or those who have a loved one(s) or family member(s) who are or have been very dependent on them, to have several fear-based links formed by others who are afraid to let go, fearful of being alone, or are scared of love being withdrawn from them, or of having to 'go without'.

Despite being deeply passionate about making a positive difference in the lives of others, many teachers working in disadvantaged communities, nurses and doctors in hospitals, social workers and police officers involved with troubled individuals often report to me that they feel exhausted from being around those they feel called to serve. When I teach them how to regularly protect and maintain their energy system, they are able to turn this situation around by learning how to give from a place of plenty, rather than trying to run on an energy supply that is empty.

Doreen Virtue, PhD talks about the energy-draining effect of negative people and places being like 'siphoning fuel at a gas station'. It has been scientifically proven that energy follows thought and directly affects our bodies.[37] The energetic connections that form between people and places are referred to by esoteric philosophies as etheric cords. These electro-magnetic energy structures attach directly to our chakras.

Be careful (of) the environment you choose for it will shape you; be careful (of) the friends you choose for you will become like them.
William Clement Stone

With the power of intention you can disconnect from negative energy sources. To do this you simply need to focus your thoughts on reinforcing the positive energy flowing between yourself and another, while at the same time consciously cutting any negative connections. This process is referred to by metaphysical energy practitioners as 'cord cutting'.

The cord cutting method that I personally follow and share with my clients strengthens positive energy exchange and releases any unhealthy associations. The process starts with the same steps as the energy-protection technique. It is also alike in that it is simple, powerful and requires only the focus of your attention and power of your intention.

Cord Cutting Method

To experience maximum benefit from this method, find a space large enough that you can comfortably swing your arms by your sides. The process works best if completed standing up, either with your eyes open or closed. (Most people find it easier to visualise with their eyes closed.)

The following steps are available as an audio recording on the book website for you to download: www.jaynemorris.com.

1. **Stand with your feet shoulder-width apart** and your arms hanging loosely by your sides. Turn your focus to your breath. Take a deep breath inward; relax your body and mind. Close your eyes if you wish.

2. **Notice any tension** you are holding in your body; if there is a feeling of tightness, contraction, stress or fatigue being held anywhere in your body, acknowledge it and imagine the tension easing away with each breath you take, gently releasing, like melting butter. With each out breath let go of anything worrying you.

3. **Observe your thoughts** as if they are clouds floating into your consciousness; just as gently as they float in, allow them to float past again, trusting that you can let go of them for now and come back to them anytime you like later.

4. **Set an intention** to connect with the life force energy within you to lovingly reinforce the flow of love between you and others and to forgive, release and heal the negative effects of any attachments that have formed, in the past or present, that have been draining your energy.

5. **Place your attention inside** and focus on how you feel in your body as you bring to mind any person or place currently depleting your energy.

6. **Locate the cord** by asking yourself: 'Where do I sense this person/place is most strongly connected to me?' Visualise

the cord that connects you energetically. Notice what thickness the cord is, what colour it has and where in your body it feels like it is attached.

7. **Allow any associated negative emotions to surface** – stress, fear, worries, and anxieties, emotions of grief, guilt, disgust, intolerance, sadness, impatience, restlessness, indecisiveness, hurt, regret, jealousy, anger and rage.

8. **Voice negative emotions out loud** – for example 'I feel anxiety flowing between us' or 'I sense jealousy when I think of you'. If you sense a body movement that accompanies the emotion permit yourself to act it out and over-exaggerate it to help release stuck emotions and mobilise energy flow.

9. **Activate energy clearing** – visualise yourself and the other person/place being surrounded in bright healing light. This light can be any colour you choose. Use your imagination to turn it up so that it is really luminous. With forgiveness for yourself and for the other person/place, release the negative charge held in the cord by handing your emotions over to be dissolved and transmuted by the healing light.

10. **Cut the cord** – imagine holding whatever cutting tool first comes to mind (for example a sword) and make a movement with your body to symbolise using it to fully release the negative cord by acting out the motion of cutting it now. Take a deep breath in and as you cut the cord, release your breath and let go with your exhalation. Affirm to yourself that all love between yourself and the other person or place will remain but that you choose now to let go of any negative energy attachments that have been draining you.

11. **Envisage surrounding your zorbing ball with a layer of protection**. Make this layer any colour and texture that

you choose. Visualise it being completely impenetrable by any negative external energies.

12. **Affirm to yourself** that only positive energy of love and peace can pass through this special layer of protection.

13. **Bring your awareness back** to the present moment with your next breath, knowing that you are now disconnected from the old negative energy that was once held between you and the other person/place and are now protected for the rest of the day/evening ahead.

Discovering Your Inner Power

The sun shines not on us, but in us.
John Muir

When was the last time that you felt connected to your own sense of personal power?

It is likely that your belief in your ability to make any kind of powerful impact in the world will have been somewhat squashed while you were busy running yourself into the ground.

Deep down I know you have a burning desire to make a positive difference because every single person I have come across who burns out seems to sense that they are here for something more. Like you, they have an inner longing to contribute in a big way. But, when we are not clear on our purpose in life, this inner drive often gets misinterpreted by our mind and turns into an addiction to doing too much, for the sake of doing something rather than nothing.

Despite working all the hours life so generously provides us, thinking this will help us to make massive progress, ironically we often only move forward marginally.

Eventually exhaustion undermines effectiveness.

Productivity increases with stress – to a point. But after that point you find yourself in the land of diminishing returns. You're working harder, but getting less quality work done. That's when burnout sets in.
Joan Borysenko

As soon as you make the conscious decision to listen and honour your body, it will start to rebuild itself. And, as your body recovers, so will your mind. Allow this self-healing to happen. It has already begun, and it is happening more quickly than you think. The more you let go and listen, the more your body's wisdom will recreate itself anew. Your mind will feel clearer, lighter and more capable of accessing the creativity connected to your inner power.

Knowing others is strength, knowing yourself is true power.
Lao Tzu

In the previous chapter I introduced several concepts and exercises relating to energy management. Your inner power is your life force energy. When you keep your energy clear, protected and radiant you are able to fully connect with your inner power and access infinite creativity, clarity and confidence.

According to metaphysical teachings the centre of your power is located just beneath your ribcage, in the area of your solar plexis. The name for this power centre in Sanskrit is Manipura, which literally translates as 'lustrous gem'. Your inner power is like a beautiful jewel, or ball of light within you, that has the potential to shine so brightly that anything you have the desire to be, do, create or have in your life is possible. Later in this chapter I will introduce you to a powerful martial arts exercise to help you boost your inner power.

The chakras are interrelated. When one chakra is out of balance it therefore influences the others and impacts on our health and well-being. According to Taoist philosophies each chakra corresponds with certain qualities or experiences and are related to the main nerve plexuses and physical organs of the human body.

Many holistic approaches are believed to be beneficial to the rebalancing of chakras. Some of the most popular include:

- Healing, such as Reiki
- Yoga
- Music
- Meditation

- Aromatherapy
- Guided visualisation

I have found all of the above to be helpful, especially when combined with talking therapies such as positive psychology and life coaching to help replace negative thinking and process emotional distress. This is because by changing our thoughts and feelings, we cause neurological changes in our brain, which impacts at a cellular level on the systems of our body, changing the functioning of our chakras and therefore impacting on our entire energy system.

Many recent studies show that talking therapies have therapeutic value and impact brain functioning and structure.
Dr John Arden

I believe it is possible to balance the chakras by identifying and healing the root cause beliefs and fear-based emotions that prevent life force energy from flowing freely between the chakras and to/from the associated nerve plexuses and physical organs.

Because burnout is an issue that the majority of clients I work with want to focus on, we often begin by exploring the root beliefs and emotions relating to this that have impacted on the balance of energy between the chakras. I help my clients to replace fear-based limiting beliefs, calm the fight-or-flight response and identify how they can replenish their physical, mental and emotional functions in order to restore their chakras.

The impact of bringing our chakras back into alignment is in some cases experienced instantly when associated health symptoms linked to adrenal fatigue simultaneously disappear. Dr David Hamilton covers this topic in great detail in his fascinating book, *How Your Mind Can Heal Your Body*, providing scientific evidence and clear explanations of the amazing healing capacity that the human body holds.

To download a complimentary audio recording of a teleseminar I hosted with Dr David Hamilton, go to the website for this book: www.jaynemorris.com.

The Mind-Body Connection

When we nourish our thoughts and emotions we stimulate neurogenesis. Neurogenesis is our ability to rewire and regenerate the circuits in our brain. Whenever we process and release old beliefs and feelings and consciously replace them with more positive, empowering ones, we cause neuroplastic changes in the brain. These changes include the creation of new neural connections which stimulate the release of chemicals into the bloodstream that then travel around the body and positively influence all of our internal organs and their connecting systems.

We now know that changing our thinking and feeling can actually manifest changes in our physical body at a cellular level.

When we move from impatience to patience, or from stressed to calm, or from one thought to another – from a thought of food to a thought of a tree, for instance – we alter the connections between neurons, produce chemicals in the brain and affect cells and systems throughout our body.

Dr David Hamilton

Our thoughts and feelings also stimulate our genes by switching them on and off, like little light switches. When a gene is switched on it produces protein. The proteins that our genes produce are vital to the immune response and the construction of new cells, skin, tendons, blood and bones.

Dr Hamilton has a theory that because the mind has been proven to influence our genes it is therefore extremely likely that the mind can also trigger the growth of stem cells because stem cells have DNA. He additionally states:

A growing number of scientists believe that some seemingly mirac-

ulous healings and spontaneous remissions (where a person recovers overnight) from serious diseases are actually the result of the movement of stem cells from bone marrow and their morphing into cells that regenerate a damaged area.

This theory is supported by award-winning scientist Ernest L. Rossi:

Many of the so-called miracles of healing via spiritual practices and therapeutic hypnosis probably occur via genetic expression in stem cells throughout the brain and body.

So, by changing your thoughts, you can truly change your life!

Strengthening Your Intuition

The only real valuable thing is intuition.
Albert Einstein

In the *Discovery* section of this book I introduced the concept of paying attention to your intuition. Your intuition is like a muscle in your body. The more you use it, the stronger it gets. If your intuition is out of shape, all it takes is a bit of practice to tone it up.

There are several different ways we can connect with our intuition. Just as some people prefer to follow the visual map on the GPS in their car, while others like to listen to the voice delivering directions, and some prefer to switch it all off and have someone walk them there, we each have favourite ways of accessing guidance too.

Learning Styles and Intuitive Abilities
In my work I have found that preferred learning styles closely match intuitive abilities. In the late 1980s Neil Fleming, a teacher

from New Zealand, developed and introduced a neuro-linguistic programming model based on his theory that as individuals we each have different preferences for the ways in which we prefer to learn and access information. Fleming and Mills (1992) suggested four modalities reflecting preferred learning styles:

Visual – prefer seeing new information visually presented as images

Aural/ Auditory – prefer listening to new information being read/spoken

Read/Write – prefer reading new information in print/written format

Kinesthetic – prefer learning by doing through carrying out a physical activity

Identifying your preferred learning style will therefore also give you a clue to your most developed channel of *clairsense,* or intuition. The term clairsense originates from the French *clair,* meaning 'clear'. It is used to describe extrasensory human awareness. There are four primary paths that this perception can take:

Clairvoyance – *clear seeing,* the ability to receive mental images, both in the mind's eye and via the world around us. Often visual learners access their intuition most easily via clairvoyance.

Clairaudience – *clear hearing,* the ability to intuit auditory messages internally, as well as messages from the external world. Aural/auditory learners tend to connect to their intuition most easily via clairaudience.

Claircognisance – *clear knowing,* the ability to receive guidance directly into your mind through ideas and thoughts that seem to simply drop into your conscious awareness. Learners who prefer to access information via written form tend to lean towards claircognisance as their dominant intuitive sense.

Clairsentience – *clear feeling*, the ability to feel and interpret messages through the body and emotions. Often referred to as 'gut feelings'. Those who like to learn by doing usually gain intuitive guidance most naturally via clairsentience.

We are all able to access intuition via all of our senses, but in the same way as we have preferred learning styles, we also tend to have a dominant intuitive sense.

Have you identified your favourite or dominant intuitive sense?

If you are still unsure or would like further confirmation, try these two quick and easy exercises:

Best Friend Test

Bring to mind your best friend. Do you:

- Visualise a picture of how she looks in your mind's eye?
- Instantly hear her as if she's next to you talking to you?
- Make a mental list of her best attributes?
- Sense in your body how you feel when you are around her?

Last Holiday

Recall your last holiday. Imagine I am in the room with you and spend about two minutes telling me about it.

Now, reflect back on the summary you have just given. Did you mainly:

- a) Talk about where you visited as if you were watching a movie in your mind or looking at snapshots of your holiday.
- b) Run through who said what to whom, the sounds of ocean/children playing/noisy traffic/ birds singing as your

key recollection.

- c) Give a debrief in bullet-point form including details of the time of year when you travelled or even the actual date/month and year, specifics about your itinerary where you went/airport you flew from/where you stayed/type of hotel/ how many days.
- d) Remember how it *felt* being away using words that summarised the experiential aspects of your holiday 'relaxing', 'exciting', 'refreshing' as if your body was back there again.

If the description you gave of your friend and/or holiday most closely matched: a) your dominant sense is clairvoyance, and you are likely to be a visual learner; b) your dominant sense is clairaudience, and your learning style is probably aural/ auditory; c) your dominant sense is claircognisance, and your preferred style of learning is likely to be via reading/writing; or d) your dominant sense is clairsentience, and you are likely to learn best kinesthetically, by doing.

The various art, coaching and meditation exercises in this book will help you to strengthen your intuitive skills by encouraging you to pay attention to your senses as you complete the activities presented here. If you are keen to take this further then I recommend Lynn Robinson's bestselling books, *Listen: Trusting Your Inner Voice in Times of Crisis*[38] and *Trust Your Gut: How the Power of Intuition Can Grow Your Business.*[39] To download a complimentary recording of my audio teleseminar featuring Lynn as my special guest, visit the website for this book: www.jaynemorris.com.

Meditation

Meditation can help you become more aware of your mind and body connection and strengthen your intuition. I have practised meditation since I was a child learning karate. We used to meditate as a class at the start and end of each training session. I did not appreciate at the time how powerful this discipline was for centring my focus and energy.

I would come into the karate class all in a rush, with my mind all over the place. The class would start with everyone lining up in front of the instructor (referred to as Sensei, which is Japanese for 'Teacher') in grade order. There was always a lot of hustle and bustle until we were asked by Sensei to sit in a kneeling position and close our eyes. A sense of calm seemed to descend upon the entire class as we all sat quietly turning our attention inwards.

By beginning each class in this way we developed a routine of quietening our minds on a regular basis. Like a muscle in the body, the more we did this, the more the muscle was strengthened. Because we sat meditating at both the start and end of each class, we soon became able to enter a meditative state quickly and easily. Some days we would sit meditating with focus on our breath for as little as one minute, and on other days for as much as 5-10 minutes.

Regardless of the length of time we sat, this time in meditation made a huge difference to our concentration levels and performance levels. It enabled us to leave the worries of the day outside the dojo door and focus more fully on our training. At the end of the session it helped us re-centre ourselves, consolidate our learning for the day and prepare for the end of the class.

Most importantly, I found that meditation helped us to stay in the present moment during our training. This is a valuable skill to apply to the practice of any sport and indeed in everyday living of our lives.

Realize deeply that the present moment is all you have. Make the NOW the primary focus of your life.
Eckhart Tolle

I continued my martial arts training throughout my teenage

years, during my time at university and my working years there-
after, as a result of which I was able to successfully meditate for
5-10 minutes each day by simply turning my attention inward,
focusing on my breath and noticing my thoughts, sensations,
and emotions, allowing them to flow through me and pass by
me.

It was not until my experience of burnout, though, that I
decided to experiment with meditation outside of the dojo
environment. Feeling frustrated at being bedridden with
extreme dizziness and fatigue, I wondered whether I might be
able to find a way forward by turning my focus within and
asking for answers. I searched online for guided meditations
with a focus on self-healing. I found them extremely insightful,
calming and uplifting to listen to.

Each day I began following guided meditations of varying
lengths, some 20 minutes, others 30 or 60 minutes. The guided
meditations helped me to observe not only the rise and fall of my
breath and the passing of my thoughts but also the sensations in
my body. I began to tap into an awareness of myself that
stretched far beyond anything I had previously encountered.

During my meditations I experienced the release of
unresolved emotional material, periods on heightened clarity,
deep insights, spontaneous solutions to problems, dream-like
visions, endorphin rushes and a connection to guidance that
appeared to come from within yet also from beyond my sense of
self.

When I discovered how listening to a guided audio
meditation or even simply playing meditation music can help
with accessing a deep meditative state, I was keen to share this
learning with others. After recovering from burnout I took
various training courses incorporating the use of guided
meditation so that I could facilitate similar meditative experiences for others.

I have now taken hundreds of clients through guided meditations that I have designed to help them let go of emotional traumas, connect with forgiveness, release resentment, receive inner guidance, clear their energy fields, balance their chakras, increase their intuition and manifest wonderful things into their lives.

Meditation Myths

If you are new to meditation I would first like to dispel some common meditation myths:

Myth #1

Meditation is only for 'New Age types'.

Meditation can be accessed by anyone, anywhere, anytime. It has been proven to positively impact concentration and improve problem-solving abilities and is becoming increasingly popular in schools and businesses.

Myth #2

Meditation is religious.

Although meditation forms part of many religious and spiritual traditions, it is not specifically a religious practice. Many of the most common meditation practises have no religious association but share the same fundamental focus of turning attention inward to observe sensations of the breath.

Myth #3

Meditation requires hours of brain training.

There are many different levels of meditation and some overlap between meditation, hypnosis and relaxation techniques. Some strict disciplines do require thousands of hours of dedication, but the basic benefits of meditation that are available to everyone do not require any lifelong devotion or complex techniques.

Myth #4
Meditation requires the ability to sit in a lotus position.

This is a traditional way of sitting for meditation in Asian countries, where people sit cross-legged for many other daily activities, too, like eating, writing and spending time with friends. But this is not a necessary position for effective meditation. It is fine to sit in a regular chair, on a stool, kneeling or even lying down.

Myth #5
Meditation means chanting over and over.

Mantra meditation is only one form of meditation; you don't have to chant to meditate. The kind of meditations featured in this book are guided meditations. You will find them in their scripted form within this book, and on the book website there are recordings of each of them with background relaxation music to assist you in slowing down thoughts and experiencing the present moment: www.jaynemorris.com.

You can also meditate without any scripted guidance or accompanying music simply by centring yourself and focusing on your breath.

Myth #6
Meditation is about making your mind go blank.

Meditation is about becoming *aware* of your thoughts, sensations and emotions, noticing how they are connected and acknowledging them. It helps us experience the present moment more fully. Meditation helps us develop mindfulness – but it is impossible for the human mind to go blank! What is possible is to slow down the amount of mental chatter and thinking that goes on so that we are able to connect with our inner sense of self.

Myth #7
Meditation is a waste of time.

This is the main excuse people come up with in order to resist trying meditation! And the mind of even the most skilled meditator will attempt to resist regular meditation practise. There are several scientifically proven benefits related to the practise of regular meditation. Some of these will be covered in the next section, *Meditation Benefits*.

Myth #8
Only vegetarians can mediate.

Becoming a vegetarian is not a prerequisite for meditation. Eating healthy high vibrational food[40] will, however, increase your ability to receive inner guidance during meditation.

Benefits of Meditation
- Increases your ability to relax
- Improves your ability to handle life's challenges calmly
- Lowers your stress levels and the levels of chemicals in your brain related to stress
- Improves your mental and emotional health
- Increases the production of chemicals in your brain that are related to longevity of well-being and quality of life
- Reduces symptoms of depression
- Helps you develop more clarity, solve problems easier and focus better
- Helps you access your creativity and inspiration
- Increases your self-awareness

- Connects you to your inner peace
- Improves the quality of your sleep
- Heightens your intuition
- Helps you feel more centred and connected to yourself and others
- Increases your energy levels and vitality

Meditation is an excellent burnout prevention and recovery tool. I highly recommend starting and ending your day with a few short minutes of meditation.

Starting the day with meditation can help you centre your energy, notice what's going on within so as without (in your internal as well as your external world), acknowledge and let go of any fears you are holding in relation to the day ahead, connect with your power, increase your creativity, become aware of any tension being held in your body so that you can release and heal, reflect upon and set positive intentions for the day ahead.

Meditation can help you connect with the essence of who you are and your infinite potential to be all you can be so that you can bring yourself more fully into your experience of each moment of the day.

Five minutes meditating in the morning literally blesses your entire day. It expands time, calms your nervous system and restores your cells. It makes forgiveness easier because it opens the heart. It interrupts the ego's proclivity for attack and defense, retrains your attitudinal musculature and delivers you to inner peace. Plus, it is free. Now our excuse for not doing it is what, exactly...?
Marianne Williamson

Ending the day with meditation can help you to replay and acknowledge what went well, express gratitude for all the blessings in your life, surround yourself in loving energy, send positive thoughts out to others, release any frustrations or resentments you have been holding in your body, receive guidance from within, connect with your inner wholeness, as well as set an intention to protect your energy before you sleep.

Burnout Root Cause Meditation

We are disturbed not by what happens to us, but by our thoughts about what happens.
Epictetus

In my private work one-on-one with clients and in workshops and retreats, I facilitate a powerful guided meditation process called *The Burnout Root Cause Meditation*. The meditation is designed to focus on finding and healing the root cause belief that has led to other associated fear-based thinking, the triggering of the fight-or-flight response, the release of stress chemicals into your body and the creation of adrenal fatigue, ultimately resulting in your experience of burnout.

The reason I use meditations to help clients identify limiting thoughts and change them is that much of the thinking governing their burnout behaviour is subconscious rather than conscious. Meditation helps them to access their subconscious mind and enlarge their perceptual view of themselves and their thought processes. In doing this they are able to enhance their self-awareness, gain invaluable insight and a more meaningful perspective of how they can improve their thinking. In changing their mindset they positively change their health, well-being and experience of life as a whole.

The Burnout Root Cause Meditation combines coaching questions, timeline therapy and regression and progression techniques that take you on a journey back in time within your mind to discover and heal your earliest memory of your root burnout belief and any associated negative emotions so that you can move beyond the belief.

The wisdom, the insight, the answer you have been waiting for… it is already inside of you.

Neale Donald Walsch

The conscious mind may not be able to identify or recall this belief or the moment at which it was formed, but through a process of deep relaxation, the subconscious mind is often able to access this information.

Facilitating a process of this type requires working with a highly skilled practitioner in order to help process and energetically remobilise previously non-permitted feelings and emotions in relation to past situations so that you can observe stuck emotions and stop be-*ing* them.

While I am limited in how much of this process I can share with you here in print form, due to the fact that you are following exercises in a book rather than working with me in person, I would like to present a simplified version of *The Burnout Root Cause Meditation* to enable you to uncover as much as possible. This process is safe and easy to follow.

The essence of this meditation is inspired by the work of Sandy Newbigging, creator of both the *Mind Detox* and *Mind Calm Methods*. To download a complimentary audio recording of a teleseminar I hosted with Sandy about the *Power of Peace* go to the website for this book: www.jaynemorris.com.

I attended several of Sandy's trainings before he formally devised what he now refers to as the *5-step method*, which he presents in his remarkable book *Heal the Hidden Cause*. Sandy introduced me to the concept of finding root cause reasons behind physical conditions, emotional issues and life problems. I was fascinated by this concept and began to experiment by blending it with the skills I acquired via advanced level trainings in energy healing, hypnotherapy, past-life regression and future-life progression.

Time and time again the *Burnout Root Cause Meditation process* has helped my clients to pinpoint the underlying, root cause thinking that has led to their burnout experience so that they can not only change it for good but also access a blank canvas on which to design the life they really want to live in the future.

I have found that when my clients uncover the key thought that has led them to experience burnout, they simultaneously regain power over their other supporting limiting thoughts and beliefs as they start to surface, ready to be challenged and changed. Think of it like pulling up potatoes in the garden. Once you get the big daddy potato out, all the smaller ones easily follow or fall away.

Before beginning this meditation it is important to relax yourself as much as possible. You may wish to first take a bath or a walk in nature before you begin. Sit somewhere that you feel safe, comfortable and will not be disturbed. Turn off your phone. Go to the toilet. Have a shawl or blanket in hand in case you feel cold; in the same way as your body temperature goes down when you sleep, it also drops during meditation.

The meditation will encourage you to connect with the internal wisdom of your body using your clairsentience, in addition to tuning in to your other intuitive channels. Depending on your preferred learning style you may choose simply to read and follow the meditation as it is written below or to listen to it as a recording. (You will find a downloadable audio version on the website for this book: www.jaynemorris.com.)

You may wish to close your eyes and focus on the images, words, phrases, inner knowing or feelings that you intuit as if experiencing them as a journey within yourself – or alternatively you may wish to keep your eyes open and have coloured pastels or a pen and some paper to hand so that you can draw or write as understanding, inspiration and guidance flows to you.

Begin by turning your focus to your breath. Take a full, deep breath all the way down into your abdomen. Allow yourself to breathe, just like a baby, by gently expanding and contracting your abdomen. Rest your awareness on each breath and allow your body to relax more and more deeply.

Notice how soft and relaxed your breathing has become. Focus on breathing in a sense of calm and breathing out any feelings of tension.

Take your attention now to the top of your head and imagine a gentle waterfall of pure, white light flowing down to the top of your head, relaxing all the little muscles of your scalp.

Feel the light flowing into your head, bathing you in warmth and relaxation. Sense that light calming and relaxing your forehead, smoothing away any lines caused by stress or tension. Soothing your eyelids, your eyes and all the little muscles around your eyes.

Sense the light relaxing the back of your head. Feel it gently easing and relaxing all of the muscles in your face and head. Feel that beautiful light flowing down now into your cheeks, moving slowly and gently into your mouth, your jaw, your teeth, your tongue. Feel a warmth softening your lips and gently relaxing your chin.

Allow the feeling of relaxation to spread into your neck, soothing all the little muscles at the front and the sides and the back of your neck. Sense waves of contentment rippling out across your shoulders, relaxing all the muscles at the top of your arms. Feel it rolling down your upper arms and elbows, right down through your lower arms, your wrists and hands and right to the tips of your fingers.

Visualise the white light spreading out across your back, easing every ligament. Releasing any tension. Relaxing and softening.

Feel a growing sense of comfort, warmth and relaxation flowing all the way down your back, spreading down through your chest and the entire trunk of your body. Send that sensation into your hips, into your stomach and your buttocks. Allow the feeling to flow down into your legs, your knees, your calves, your ankles and right the way down to the tips of your toes.

Focus your attention on the light flowing through you, all the way from the top of your head, down across your face, down your throat and chest, down into your lower abdomen, into the top of your legs and right down to your toes. Then send it back up your legs, all the way along your spine, up to your neck and head, over the top of your head and back down your face again, back down through your arms and body, down through your hips, your legs, across your knees, down your shins.

With each exhalation release any tensions to this white light and sense any stress, worry, or fears being transmuted by this light. Sense that you are safe and protected by this light. As you breathe in, breathe in the sense of peace and protection that the light gives you.

Set an intention now to uncover and begin healing the root cause of the belief you have been holding that has ultimately led to your burnout experience.

Ask yourself the question: 'What is the thought that I have been holding that has ultimately led to my burnout experience?'

Allow the answer to flow to you via your intuitive senses. You may notice a feeling in your body of tightness or contraction, of openness or expansion, of warmth or cold, of pain or peace or become aware of symptoms of illness.

Ask your body what it wants to communicate with you; it may respond with further physical sensations, or the answer may come as images in your mind's eye, a whispering of an inner voice, or an understanding that simply drops into your conscious awareness.

Give yourself permission to connect now with the higher learning you need to know. Ask what thoughts you need to change for your highest good. Wait for the response.

Ask what you can release from your life in order to clear and increase your energy. Wait for the response.

Ask what one thing you can know now, that had you known in the past, you would never have experienced patterns of burnout in first place.

Wait for the response and state this new belief back to yourself.

This is the belief that you now need to hold in order to move beyond your experience of burnout and create a life of well-being, passion and purpose for your future.

Feel the positive energy of this new belief. If this knowing had a colour, what would it be?

Imagine that colour flowing all the way around your body, replenishing every cell and reenergizing every level of your being.

Know that you can connect to the energy of this new belief at any time to help you move forward and make positive change in your life.

Take your non-dominant hand and place it over the part of your body where you feel this new belief residing the strongest. Know that just by placing your hand here in the future you can instantly reaffirm this belief to yourself and positively affect your energy.

Return your focus to your breath. Take three deep breaths and bring your awareness back to your surroundings. Stretch your body and feel yourself physically and mentally returning fully to the present moment.

Uncover Your Brightest Potential

You are the power in your world!
Louise Hay

If you have been completing all of the exercises presented in this book so far then you are now likely to be feeling well on the road to recovery from burnout. The next section of the book will help you to focus on your future so you can uncover who you truly want to be from now on, so you can re-energise your life and develop sustainable strategies for success in order to continue to shine at your brightest potential.

Much of what I have covered up until this point has been internally focused work based on recalibrating your energy and mindset. It is also important to nourish your system with good food, sufficient sleep and an exercise system.

You may already feel super charged and ready for anything, but equally your inner guidance may be hinting that you still need to take time to rest and recuperate. While rapid recovery is completely possible, it is important to follow your intuition with your recovery and not push yourself to do too much too soon.

The more willing you are to surrender to the energy within you, the more power can flow through you.
Shakti Gawai

I recommend following the next exercise when you feel ready to surrender and truly open to the full potential power you hold within. *The Power Shout* is one of my favourite techniques to boost inner power is an energising shout that I have adapted from my training in martial arts.

Your inner power holds the key to living your life feeling energised and with a purpose.

Your body will give you access to this unlimited source of internal power but only if you mind promises that you will prioritise self-care from now on. It is like the principle I mentioned earlier in the book of first putting on your own oxygen mask before helping others on an aeroplane. You need to take care of yourself before you can take care of anything else in your life.

Are you willing to do that?

If the answer is yes, then you are ready to read on and discover how to connect with your inner power so that you can shift your life story, connect with your purpose and make a miraculous impact not just in your life, but in the lives of others and on the world.

Inside of you is the power to be, do, have and create anything you can imagine. *Anything.* You were born with everything you need to become your own answer to an amazing life. When you tap in to your inner power, trust your intuition and take action in alignment with your biggest and brightest vision for yourself, you will astound yourself!

If you think you're too small to have an impact, try going to bed with a mosquito.
Anita Roddick

I spent most of my early childhood in Scotland. Both sides of my family live on the west coast. When I was small my parents moved to England because my father accepted a new job based in Bristol. I was six years old at the time and was in my first year of primary school. I remember being excited about the move and really enjoying my first experience of flying on an aeroplane and getting to choose a new bedroom when we arrived at our new home. I was also excited about starting at a new school and was met with great kindness by my new headmaster on my first day.

I liked my new surroundings and was keen to fit in and make new friends. My Scottish accent must have stuck out because the children teased me about it. I anxiously tried to change the way I spoke so that I would sound more like them. As I moved up through the school I lost my accent, and this difference between us was forgotten. I had managed to temporarily overcome the situation by hiding part of my identity. I say temporarily because similar situations kept presenting themselves throughout my childhood and teenage years.

I was a conscientious student. I worked hard and got good grades. It was not considered 'cool' to achieve top marks in class, so I used to hide my work in order to avoid teasing. This worked temporarily, but the more I tried to hide parts of myself, the more I seemed to attract challenges in the form of bullying.

Perhaps 'tall poppy syndrome', the criticism or attack of people on account of talents or achievements that distinguish them, is something you've been on the receiving end of yourself at some stage in your life?

Standing tall and allowing one's own talents to shine means risking being the first to be cut down, or to receive ridicule from others, often stemming from their own insecurities.

My experiences of bullying during my early teenage years in particular made many of my school days miserable. I did not know how to handle incidents when they arose. There was one girl in particular whom I knew purposefully stirred up the significant majority of the trouble I encountered, yet when I approached her alone without an audience, hoping to resolve any issue she had with me one-to-one, she denied having any real issue with me.

The advice of my parents was always to ignore things, and in my martial arts training I was taught never to be the first to attack. I respected these teachings and did my best to believe the saying 'sticks and stones may break my bones but names will never hurt me' – all the while wishing there was some way I could make it stop.

After several years of torment continuing on a regular basis, the same girl spread a rumor that lead to me being attacked by two of the most physically intimidating girls in my school year. It was the first time I had been forced to physically defend myself.

One lunchtime I was leaving the school library and walked out to find the two girls waiting for me in the corridor. One of them launched for my neck as if intending to grab me. I don't remember having time to think, let alone be afraid; almost instinctively I used a combination of karate techniques to defend myself.

As I walked away the second girl came after me and also tried to attack me. Again I defended myself, and from somewhere deep within I additionally found the power to verbally tell her to back off.

I felt like I had finally been able to stand up for myself and positively demonstrate and assert my inner power.

The bullying stopped. Once and for all.

Since that day, something had shifted. I began to rediscover my own sense of unique identity and no longer felt I had to hide. I felt more comfortable and confident expressing myself with authenticity and never again encountered any further incidents of bullying.

When I moved up to sixth form I set up a 'Beat the Bully' club to help partner younger students in the school with a more senior student who acted as their mentor and helped diffuse situations similar to that which I had encountered. It is hard for teachers to help students overcome bullying, whereas an older sibling, friend or mentor can make all the difference.

I was very fortunate that I had self-defence skills to draw upon when faced with a physical attack. To this day I believe it to be invaluable to equip children with the knowledge of how to protect their energetic, emotional and physical well-being, in addition to overcoming defensive self-depreciation, and instead be confident in expressing their talents and abilities.

Upon reflection, being bullied as a child actually helped me to develop awareness and resilience of the need for personal protection. But, it was a very hard way to learn such a lesson, and my heart goes out to every child facing such a challenge.

Bullying is an issue for many adults, too, and can completely destroy career progression. Workplace bullying or harassment can happen face-to-face or via letter, email, phone or via the spreading of malicious rumours. It can take various forms, for example denying someone opportunities that they are entitled to, picking on someone, regularly undermining someone or other unfair treatment. Often it is related to jealousy or discrimination concerning age, sex, sexual orientation, gender, disability, race, religion or other beliefs.

Overcoming bullying as an adult in many ways presents the same challenge as when faced with the issue as a child or adolescent. To rise above the harassment it is important to regain your sense of self-worth and self-confidence, stand in your power and assert yourself.

Sometimes it can be possible to resolve workplace harassment issues by informally addressing the bully and attempting to discuss the situation. If the problem persists then it is advisable to speak with someone more senior, approach HR for advice or seek support from a trade union representative. It is also worth exploring the option of making a formal complaint following your employer's grievance procedure. Legal action is also an option if things continue to escalate.

If you have been struggling with self-confidence or simply want to increase you sense of inner power, there is a simple, yet extremely effective martial arts technique that can help you reconnect with your inner brilliance.

I drew upon this very technique on the day I stood tall and asserted myself. I have continued to use it ever since, whenever I want to realign with my power, passions and purpose – and, I have introduced it to thousands of people all over the world.

The Japanese refer to this technique as 'Ki-Ai', which literally means 'energy out'. If you have ever watched a martial arts movie then you will no doubt have noticed a lot of strange sounds and noises being made whenever there are fight scenes. Despite being exaggerated for the benefit of making an inter-esting film, these noises actually serve a purpose of helping the martial artist to focus their attention and amplify the impact of their efforts.

The 'Ki-Ai' is essentially an energy expansion and direction tool that combines focus, breath and energy expansion with a shout. At first, people tend to feel quite uncomfortable and self-conscious when I ask them to experiment with making such a sound. But, once they have tried it a few times, they soon relax into the technique and are often surprised by the powerful affect it has on them.

I now lovingly refer to this technique as the *Power Shout*, because on several occasions, it has helped me to stand in my power and overcome obstacles.

At the stage of my life when I reached burnout and had disconnected from my own sense of inner strength, I used the *Power Shout* to help me reconnect with my inner potential. This enabled me to make powerful changes in order to truly value and honour self-care, embrace my passions and follow my purpose. Connecting with my inner power after burnout helped me gain the clarity I needed to develop sustainable strategies for my future.

When you connect with your inner power, you connect with inner wisdom. It can help you prioritise peace, positively radiate from the inside out, and supports the manifestation of all that you feel inspired to create in your life.

The key steps to follow in order to learn the *Power Shout* are outlined below. Alternatively you can find a video version on the webpage for this book: www.jaynemorris.com.

Power Shout Exercise

1. **Stand with your feet apart**, knees slightly bent, and relax your body.
2. **Close your eyes and take three deep breaths.** Turn your attention inwards. Breathe in through your nose and allow each breath to drop right down to the bottom of your abdomen. Fill your lungs completely with your in-breath, and as you exhale, expel all the stale air you've been holding inside.
3. **Sense the energy at your core**, the area just beneath your rib cage. You may sense this as a certain colour or shape and feel it moving. Notice how positive and energising it feels and imagine expanding it slowly to fill your entire body. Then expand it so that it completely surrounds you as if you are in a zorbing ball filled with your energy.

4. **Power-up your energy** with your next breath by connecting with that sense of energy in your sternum, and as you breathe out, expel the energy as fast and powerfully as you can, with your breath. It will make a strange sound. To increase your power, try verbalising the sound five times, making a deep noise 'ee-ah' each time you breathe out, progressively getting louder and louder each time. In Japanese, this sound is called 'Ki-Ai' which means 'energy out' or 'energy focus'.

The sound 'ee-ah' connects you with your inner power in an extremely calming way. Studies have shown that our heart rate actually decreases when 'ee-ah' sounds are repeated.[41]

5. **Believe in your inner power** – the energy you have connected with contains all you need to stay fresh, focused and revitalised. You can connect back in with it any time you need to gain clarity, recharge or renew your sense of purpose. When you are connected with your inner power you inspire others to step into their power and potential too. Believe in the power of you today and be your brightest, most brilliant and nurtured self.

The Power Shout technique has helped me feel absolutely incredible from inside. My world opened up and expanded because my vision of where I am going has become so clear and now seems to be expanding even more and more.

Before working with Jayne my feeling was that it was hard to balance both love and business. I thought that life was dependent on choosing one over the other. Since working with Jayne I have realised that in truth a balance of both is possible... There has been a big change in the way I approach my life and business, because I believe I can have everything that is important to me.

I now believe I can enjoy the process of life and that all I need is belief, a clear vision, patience, and a little creativity. I already have all of those, so in turn, I can see great times ahead! I feel very happy and my world has absolutely been revolutionised as I have great belief in myself, in my life ahead, and that my vision is already in fulfillment. Thank you Jayne very much for the inner power and inspiration you have given back to me.

Adam White, Owner AW Personal Training, London

Blasting Through Blocks

Have you ever noticed that just before making a big break-through you consider giving up because the path ahead seems blocked by boulders?

Often, just when we are tempted to give up, our biggest break-through is waiting right around next corner.

This chapter addresses some of the common stumbling blocks that can hold people back from overcoming burnout.

False Notions

Mental stress does not come from the problems that beset us, but from the irrational and false notions we have about them.
John Perry

It is our beliefs about incidents and events that determine how we respond to them. Some people have a tendency to magnify things and blow them up out of proportion: 'I failed my promotion interview – my career is in ruins'; 'I missed the train – this is terrible'; 'We didn't win the contract – it's the end of the world'.

We can also do this when we predict negative future outcomes: 'I am going to really embarrass myself in this meeting'; 'If I make a mistake everyone will laugh at me'; 'I bet everyone thinks I am an idiot'.

In order to change irrational thoughts to rational ones when a stressful situation arises, take a deep breath, relax your body and mind, pause for a moment and evaluate what *actually* happened. Notice that the event or situation is not life threatening. This will calm you down and help you put things into perspective. Become aware of how you perceive the situation. Are you viewing it as negative? Change your thoughts so that you see it differently. Choose to see it positively.

For example, the next time you are stuck in traffic (and instead of telling yourself that it is a total disaster), reframe the situation as a positive opportunity – see it as a chance to daydream about your next holiday or listen to that language CD you've been meaning to listen to.

Adopting the right attitude can convert a negative stress into a positive one.
Professor H Selye

By becoming aware of your perception of things you will able to choose to minimize rather than magnify the negativity of individual situations and predict successful outcomes rather than negative ones. The cumulative effect of doing this will be an inner sense of calm and well-being rather than one of overwhelm.

Having It All as a Woman

Pioneering editor of *Cosmopolitan* magazine, Helen Gurley Brown, first coined the term 'having it all'. She passionately believed that women were entitled to a great career, family, and love life – which of course, we are!

I have attended several conferences and events where the topic of women being driven by a constant pursuit of 'having it all' has been explored in open discussions between speakers, panelists and delegates.

While I believe it is possible to 'have it all' in the sense of enjoying all aspects of one's life and feeling fulfilled by one's career, love life and family relationships, I think it is important to distinguish that it is not possible to give 100% of one's energy to everything simultaneously. There is a difference between having it all and being everything to everyone.

It is important to share responsibilities and be willing to accept help. Having it all does not mean 'doing it all'.

Attempting to do it all at the same time is where many women trip themselves up. For instance, despite recent studies indicating that the gap in employment rates between men and women (with and without children) has narrowed over the last fifteen years,[42] studies also indicate that the gap in division of housework has remained largely unchanged.[43] In the UK women were recently found responsible for twice as much housework as men[44], and in the USA less than 10% of working couples said that they equally shared household chores.[45]

This is not the only issue preventing them from advancing. Recent research by McKinsey in the United States[46] stated that:

Young women, just like young men, start out with high ambitions. But while they never lose belief in their own abilities, they do frequently turn down advancement opportunities because of commitments outside work, risk aversion to positions that demand new skills, or a desire to stay in roles that they feel provide personal meaning. A reluctance to promote themselves is also an issue.

Although women have made great strides in attaining equality in the workplace, the corporate and political landscape is still predominantly influenced and informed by males. It has traditionally been structured by men and therefore naturally promotes male-orientated values and behaviours. In order to succeed in male-dominated environments, women have had to demonstrate their ability to perform 'like men'.

For several decades women have attempted to emulate men as a means to gaining equality in the workplace. While this arguably helped women progress in the past it is now hindering women from creating the careers they want for their future.

The world of work has changed significantly since the early 20th century when Western women began to fight for equal rights, yet women continue to experience challenges in advancing their careers to senior leadership level. Recent global statistics show that women hold only 20% of seats in government and far less than 20% of executive officer positions and board level seats. A report issued in 2008 by the Equality and Human Rights Commission suggested that 'at the current rate of change it would take over 70 years to achieve gender-balanced board-rooms in the UK'.

There is clear evidence that having women in leadership results in better decision-making.[47] Companies with a strong female representation at senior management level perform better than those without.[48] Gender-diverse leadership groups are more able to consider issues in a rounded, holistic way and offer greater attention to detail.[49]

Women think, feel and behave differently than men. These differences are what make women so valuable in leadership positions but are also ironically what prevent women from breaking through the glass ceiling, regardless of qualifications and achievements.

Women are noted as being more nurturing, empathic and responsive, whereas men are perceived to be more action-orien-tated and task-focused.[50] It is often said that women 'take care' whereas men 'take charge'.[51] It is my intention to highlight this as a strength that women innately hold, rather than a stereotype that should hold women back.

The very qualities that make women great leaders need to be actively acknowledged, appreciated and encouraged at every stage of the pipeline, from entry level through to senior management.

Many of the high-achieving women I work with burn out because they feel over extended, not just in one area, but across all aspects of their lives. They don't feel sufficiently supported either at home or in the workplace. Rather than asking or demanding the help they need, they develop 'Superwoman Syndrome'[52] in attempt to overcome support deficiencies.

Superwoman Syndrome is not sustainable. I believe it is one

of the key underlying reasons why there are currently so few women in leadership positions.

Director of the European Sustainability Academy, Sharon Jackson left the electronics industry after spending 15 years working for large multinational companies at a very senior level:

I burnt out. I completely crashed. I went to bed for 2 months and couldn't get up. I couldn't make a decision. I couldn't decide if I wanted tea or coffee. That was the most important thing that happened to me in my whole life. Because, when I did get out of bed I wasn't superwoman anymore. Since I've stopped being superwoman my life has become super.

In 2000 I had a moral dilemma about what the electronics industry was doing to the planet and to the people working for us. At that time we had people dropping like flies, dying of heart attacks through stress... I was taking this issue to our board and they were replying, 'Don't be so silly Sharon, that's the way our business is run'... Eventually I felt that I couldn't give my business card to someone without feeling physically sick. I resigned...

When I left that corporation I lost my identity. I lost my BMW, I lost my five-star hotel, I lost all of my first-class travel... I was nobody... I was not a top executive anymore. I found it really difficult...

I had to rebuild myself around a different style of leadership. My style of leadership was authoritative, command and control, impressing, all about impressing... I probably spent most days going to work not being me.... fitting in with the norms of that culture and organisation... I had to rebuild myself... I learned that the way we give our sense, the way we receive sense from people and how we allow interpretation of leadership is far more important than the authoritative command and control....

For the past 13 years I have been developing myself as a leader... in losing my command and control I have reached a new leadership, which has allowed people to come to me in their own time... I've made myself very available... All kinds of enriching things have emerged as a result.

In order for women to establish themselves equally in positions of leadership, the balance of values within our corporate culture needs to shift away from competitive command and control leadership towards a more collaborative, open and authentic way of conducting business.

Instead of women being forced to choose between their family and their career, we need to find ways for women to continue contributing towards both, without being over extended and without feeling like they need to sacrifice one in order to have the other.

For both men and women to enjoy successful careers and satisfying personal lives it is necessary for us to find new ways of supporting each other in the workplace and at home. In doing this perhaps we can 'be' more fully present in all areas of our lives rather than running an uphill race to try and 'have' it all.

Individuals and organisations both need to take action in order to make this happen.

McKinsey's *Women Matter 2010* report highlighted the following ways organisations can support gender diversity and increase the number of women accessing senior-level positions:

Management Awareness

- Ensure top management are committed to improving gender diversity by placing it on the group CEO's strategic agenda.
- Set quantitative targets for women's representation in leadership positions.
- Ensure company culture is consistent with gender

diversity objectives.

- Take action to increase men's awareness of gender diversity issues.

Coaching and Development

- Invest in women's development programme including networking, leadership and mentoring.
- Use external coaches and implement programmes to increase proportion of potential women leaders.

Human Resource Management

- Revise human resources processes and policies so that flexible working is not penalised, different leadership styles are recognised and rewarded.
- Take action to overcome gender biases in appraisals and recruitment.
- Address root cause issues when top women performers want to leave and explore retention.

Flexible Working

- Increase logistical flexibility by promoting remote working.
- Provide greater career flexibility.
- Devise a policy to schedule meetings only during business hours.
- Establish a support system to assist in smooth transition before, during, and after maternity leave.
- Guarantee to keep similar or better position for women returning from leave of absence.
- Provide regular individual contact with human resource departments or management to define career path.

Support for Families

- Offer in-house childcare facilities.

- Provide services for sick children (for example, nurse in attendance at home).
- Provide mobility support with finding schools for children.
- Provide job search programmes to support spouse or partner.

This is not an exhaustive list of what can be done to help shift corporate culture and better support more women in becoming tomorrow's leaders, but it is a good starting point from which organisations can draw inspiration to help them make positive change and commit to raising women's representation in the workforce.

One of the key elements in enabling women to succeed at senior level and seeing them *stay* there is the provision of sufficient support to allow them to devote time and attention to their families, not just their jobs.

Many women choose not to advance their careers because they value their family more than their employer does. This has to change. Organisations need to value the contribution that women make, not just in business or politics, but to society as a whole when they are given the opportunity to be both great leaders and great mothers. It should not be about choosing to be one or the other.

When former Director of Policy Planning at the State Department, Anne-Marie Slaughter left her two-year public-service leave from Princeton University she stepped down from her position of power as fast as possible. When people asked why she had left government, she explained that she'd come home 'not only because of Princeton's rules (after two years of leave, you lose your tenure), but also because of my desire to be with my family and my conclusion that juggling high-level government work with the needs of two teenage boys was not possible'.

I had the pleasure of discussing this topic with Lady Lynn Forster de Rothschild, CEO of El Rothschild, whom I invited to join me for a teleseminar on this topic.[53] She impressed upon our audience that women are able to have it all when we change the emphasis of the goal we are working towards from one of *having* to one of *being*.

> *'Can we have it all?' is a loaded question that we should not impose on ourselves. The ultimate goal of life is not about having, it's about being. The ultimate goal is about being comfortable in yourself, it is about knowing that your life has been lived with integrity and that your family and friends can count on you. I believe life is about being, not having... Can we have a great career and can we have a great family? The answer is unequivocally – yes.*
>
> Lady Lynn Forster de Rothschild

When women focus on caring both for themselves and for others we can truly come together and move forward as leaders for the next generation. The change begins with every woman being the change she wants to see in the world and leading by example.

To close the leadership gap we need to shift our definition of success from money, power and competition towards well-being and collaboration. In doing this more women will be able to access and maintain positions of power, and most importantly, be able to play their part in creating a new, more balanced and caring global community.

Here are some suggestions for how you can begin making this change for yourself:

Within your home life

- Take care of your own needs as a priority so that you can support your family from a place of plenty, rather than running on empty.
- Ask for help rather than trying to do everything by

yourself.

- Have an open dialogue with your partner, family, flat mates about equal distribution of tasks around the home.
- Outsource as many routine tasks that provide you with little pleasure as possible, within your financial means.
- Lower the bar on perfectionism.
- Address feelings of guilt.
- Devote more time to *be* more present to the experience of your life.
- Avoid criticising other women; instead acknowledge that every woman is doing the best she can do in any given moment.
- Avoid comparing yourself to other women and indulging in self-criticism.

Within your career

- Be a shade braver when opportunities for career advancement become available. If a new role requires acquiring new skills, have greater faith in your ability to acquire them and ask for support in developing them.
- Re-establish boundaries with your workload and working hours.
- Practice saying no. Commit to leaving work on time. Take your full paid leave entitlement.
- Ask to renegotiate your salary, benefits, work setup, or workload if you feel you are not feeling satisfied with your current arrangement.
- Request career coaching.
- Attend networking events and actively seek out exciting advancement opportunities.
- Approach someone in a senior position within your organisation or via a programme like The Aspire Foundation[54] about being your mentor.
- Avoid self-criticism and criticism of other women.

- Ask for more flexible working arrangements.

Having It All as a Man

You thought that men already had it all? Well no, not really.

A man's education begins a hundred and fifty years before he is born.
Oliver Wendell Holmes

Many men are operating on the manual given to him by his grandfather, which exhorted that he should push, strive, work hard, and provide for his family. As a child he was unlikely to have guidance around giving value to the joys of parenting. Fortunately, we are starting to challenge the outdated framework of fatherhood, and men are embracing the opportunity to more fully participate in family life.

Since the 1960s hospitals in many western countries have permitted men to attend the birth of their children. Yet, it has taken us several decades to pass laws that permit men to take paternity leave after the birth so that they can actually spend time with their children and support their partners. In most parts of the world we still have a long way to go in order to extend this leave so that it can truly have a significant impact. Some countries, including the US, still have no national law mandating paid time off for new parents, but fortunately others, like Sweden and Norway, are well ahead of the others and setting shining examples of the benefits that this can bring.

The time is ripe to move toward a new evolutionary agenda – not to reform but to transform.
Barbara Marx Hubbard

Deputy Prime Minister Nick Clegg announced the inspiration he has taken from the Scandinavian countries that are leading the way and has committed to reform parental leave legislation in the UK from 2015. While it is wonderful that such reforms are currently underway we still have a long way to go before men have an equal entitlement and feel it is acceptable for them to take their full amount of leave. Now is the time to start transforming employment frameworks to better support modern families.

Kaite Douglas, Legal Director of the International Law Firm, Pinsent Masons, commented that although the number of men taking paternity leave in the UK rose by 14% between 2011-2012, it is still largely unused by the vast majority of male employees in her firm:

Despite the Government's determination to encourage fathers to take paternity leave, many men still do not exercise their right. They may balk at the prospect because they fear that their doing so is still frowned upon by employers.

I believe it is vital that we take action to positively change perceptions of men taking paternity leave in order to support men to be more actively involved as parents at each stage of childhood, not just when their children are first born.

In my experience of working with men who have burnt out, many state that the high price they paid for the endless hours of overwork was not only the negative impact this had on their health but the family relationships that broke down as a result. Years of late nights at the office and weekends working away meant they missed meals with their wife; bedtime stories, sports events and school plays with their children - even family holidays.

At 1 or 2am I was heading for home. The more tired I was, the more I pushed myself. When my wife tried to caution me, I responded with irritation... During this period not only wasn't I listening to myself, I wasn't listening to anyone...Things continued this way for months as I continued to deny that anything was wrong despite my lingering cold, my fatigue, and my constant irritability. During the Christmas holiday my wife insisted that we take a vacation with the children... I felt I should go to make up for all the time I had spent away from home. My wife made the hotel and plane reservations. All I had to do the night before we left was pack my own clothes, but when I dragged myself through the door at 2am, I was too exhausted to do anything except fall into bed. I told my wife that I would pack in the morning, but in the morning I couldn't get up. I slept for two solid days and ruined the family vacation.

Dr Herbert Freudenberger

I believe it is no coincidence that a number of men who divorce and remarry regularly wine and dine with their new wives, visit luxurious locations and spend more time with the children they have in their first marriage. Many want to make up for what they neglected the first time around.

If you share in your kids' lives and give them a chance to take part in yours, you will have a much better relationship with them ... If you are struggling to juggle your home life with your career commitments, both can suffer. Part of the solution may be to treat time with your family as a priority. When you're facing an avalanche of appointments, book time to spend with your family – put it in your work diary.

Richard Branson

Deloitte Consulting LLP Chairman and CEO Jim Moffatt discovered that in stepping away from his work and spending 'much-needed time' with his family, not only were the benefits felt in his home life and relationship with his children but also by his employees. In order to leave his desk and be with his family, he needed to trust his top people. In his absence they did not fail to deliver, and as a result he has never looked back. He now maintains that:

A true leader steps back, trusts his or her people, and allows them to succeed… By taking a break from the day-to-day operations, not only was I spending some much-needed time with my family, but I was also able to focus on the bigger picture of where we were and where our business was heading.

For both men and women to truly 'have it all' we need flexibility in the way we work so that we can take better care of our own needs and those of our children. This is vital not only to help prevent burnout of the workforce, but also to prevent the burnout of our children. Many parents who overwork and overschedule themselves force their children to do the same. In failing to identify their own need for self-care they fail to identify the needs their children have too.

When we master the art of seeing self-care as selfless rather than selfish we begin to regain our energy, feel alive again, be more present with our children, and when we are more present with our kids we can better support them emotionally and spiritually.
Heather Chauvin

When we are out of tune with ourselves and our own needs it is difficult for us to stay attuned to the true needs of our children. Many parents overschedule their children because they become overly focused on providing them with access to a vast array of activities that were not available when they were children. Some get caught up in comparing themselves with other parents and underlying inter-parental competition. Others become obsessed with after-school tutoring to support academic achievement. Many parents also subconsciously prioritise work above caring for their child themselves and develop a schedule of extracurricular activities to 'take care' of their children on their behalf.

The outcome is children who are as exhausted as their parents, have no downtime, no opportunity to experience boredom or explore spontaneous play, and are emotionally lacking because interactions within their family are suppressed.

When there is no time for family dinner, no time to sit and talk, play games, or have unstructured play, what we are teaching our kids when they are overscheduled is that their worth is determined by their performance – and that's not healthy.

Julie Hanks

In 2003 the UK government introduced an initiative titled *Every Child Matters*. The main aims are for every child, whatever their background or circumstances, to receive the support they need to stay safe and healthy, enjoy and achieve, have economic well-being and the opportunity to make a positive contribution in society.

'Having it all' as a child is about experiencing each of these things in balance, in addition to receiving the unconditional love of their parent(s)/caregiver(s) and the freedom to play and be a child.

Our culture sends parents a message that unstructured leisure hours waste valuable time. Play appears frivolous, taking away from the future success of your child, in a society that places a premium not only on being successful but also on being a star.

Stacey DeBroff

Whilst encouraging our children to fulfill their potential by fostering their self belief and supporting their natural talents is very positive, preventing them from truly being children by putting pressure on them to excel from a young age is harmful, not helpful, to their overall development and well-being.

If you identify with your own burnout tendencies spilling over to your children, consider how you giving to yourself will in turn benefit them.

Any time you find yourself struggling to listen to your intuition and prioritise self-care, remind yourself that in order to truly give to your children you first need to give to yourself. Remember that children live what they learn. Be kinder to yourself and you will automatically find it easier to be gentle with your children and encourage your children to be gentle with themselves too.

You are worth anything it takes to stay rested, happy, and deeply tuned into the people you serve.
Nancy Kline

Compulsive Comparison

The reason we struggle with insecurity is because we compare our behind the scenes with everyone else's highlight reel.
Steve Furtick

Whenever we measure or evaluate ourselves against other people we become insecure, disconnect from our inner brilliance and stop taking intuitively guided action. This phenomenon is commonly referred to as 'compulsive comparison'.

If you notice you have a tendency to constantly compare yourself to others, be gentle with yourself. Whenever this tendency shows up, instead of allowing it to stir up jealousy, competitiveness or paranoia, play with the silly suggestions it makes and use those suggestions to diffuse situations that you find yourself in. Here are some examples:

- The next time someone stands out as being somehow 'better' than you, compliment him or her on one thing you genuinely admire about them.

- When something goes 'wrong' and you start beating yourself up about how brilliantly someone else would have succeeded with the same thing, stop – regain your sense of humor and share your failure with someone who will help you see the funny side of it.
- If you are meeting someone successful and start to feel anxiety rising up inside you, remind yourself that they are human, just like you. Imagine them hanging out in their pajamas on a Sunday morning, just like you do. There, they don't seem so scary now – do they?
- The next time you find yourself deliberating over a decision before seeking a second opinion that deep down you know you do not really need, check in with your gut feeling and trust that it is enough.
- Whenever you feel the urge to criticise someone else or start to imagine everyone else is criticising you, start finding something to admire instead. See *Stop Complaining* on page 233 for a useful exercise to help overcome this.

Perfectionism

Many schools and academies in the UK have become extremely competitive and place a great amount of pressure on students to meet the very highest academic standards. As a result our children are conditioned to push themselves to achieve the highest results that they are capable of at school and university so that they can go on to secure the best jobs possible upon graduation.

When high expectations are held of us from an early age we can start to develop an internal drive to meet the standards set for us and feel chronically unhappy or dissatisfied if we don't achieve the level of success we set out to accomplish. This develops into perfectionism in adulthood and results in the relentless quest for excellence.

Although not all perfectionists are necessarily high achievers, perfectionism propels many people forward to push themselves in often unhealthy ways in personal, professional and sporting pursuits.

Signs of Perfectionism

- Highly critical of oneself and others
- Takes criticism personally
- Sets hugely ambitious goals and stops at nothing to achieve them
- Feels empty or unsatisfied if expectations are not exceeded or first-class results are not achieved
- Always moving the goal posts to go above and beyond targets
- Finds it difficult to open up and be completely authentic with others
- Sets such high standards that consistent success becomes impossible to achieve, resulting in shame and guilt
- Lack of patience
- Workaholism

Perfectionism can prevent you from following your true desires and keep you chained to your desk, working far longer hours than would be necessary if you were willing to take the pressure off yourself and accept things being completed when they are 'good enough'. Of course, there are times when paying incredible attention to detail is essential, but investing that level of concentration to every project you work on leads to overwhelm and is not a sustainable strategy for success.

Perfectionism can prevent us from acknowledging the best in ourselves because our attention becomes focused on overly obsessing with the worst in ourselves. As a result perfectionists often beat themselves up with negative self-talk and self-defeating behaviour.

For some perfectionists an overwhelming fear of failure can cause procrastination and result in risk-adversity. This inhibits self-esteem, can lead to intense fear of rejection and of making mistakes, and can result in all kinds of psychological, behavioural, and physiological issues ranging from depression, withdrawal and chronic fatigue to eating disorders.

Fear of failure can result in indecisiveness and prevent people from moving forward, not just in their careers but in other areas of their lives too. When procrastination due to perfectionism perpetuates it can lead to severe hoarding issues, time management problems, relationship ruptures, intimacy issues, excessive worry and financial concerns.

Judy Hobbs[55] former executive for a global tax, auditing and advisory firm, felt that fear of failure that had held her back from following her true passions and starting her own holistic healthcare business. She also identified that perfectionist tendencies had caused her to push herself since she was a child. In her career she had felt so unfulfilled that she began to experience each day a continuous uphill struggle to keep going.

Eventually Judy burned out. When she approached me about working together she said she was experiencing an 'identity crisis'. She had spent the previous six months signed off sick from work. When she described what had been going on over the past few years she highlighted excessively exercising to help her switch off. 'I used to run until I was too tired to think' she told me. Surviving on just 4 hours of sleep per night, she eventually became so physically and emotionally exhausted that she lost all confidence and felt 'helpless and hopeless'.

I helped Judy uncover the root cause thinking behind her fear of making mistakes so that she could permit herself to follow her heart and re-adjust her approach to risk taking. Now Judy has completely transformed the way she approaches exercise, relationships and work. She is running her own business and says she can 'barely contain her excitement' because she is so 'upbeat and motivated'. She has released her fear of failure and says her new favourite quote is:

I've learned so much from my mistakes... I'm thinking of making some more.

Cheryl Cole

If you struggle to take action for fear of 'getting it wrong', producing 'average' results or appearing a fool, practice becoming an imperfectionist by allowing yourself to do something 'good enough'. Getting *something* done is better than getting *nothing* done.

Give yourself permission to lower the bar and allow for mistake making.

I make mistakes like the next man. In fact, being – forgive me – rather cleverer than most men, my mistakes tend to be correspondingly huger.

J.K. Rowling, *Harry Potter and the Half-Blood Prince*

Wherever possible practice patience instead of perfectionism.

Remind yourself daily that great things can be achieved by taking small steps, making mistakes, permitting playfulness, indulging in your passions and allowing for rest and relaxation along the way.

Extreme Perseverance

Believing in yourself and getting back on your feet when you have experienced a failure or when life knocks you down are important qualities. I encourage people to affirm to themselves that they 'can do it' – except when they 'can't do it' any longer, at least not without first taking a break to rest and refuel.

Admitting defeat can be difficult for many people who pride themselves in achieving the impossible, especially when the going gets tough. Perseverance can be a great personal trait; but only when you have sufficient gas left in your tank to keep going. Extreme perseverance is not healthy because it requires running on reserves, which rarely pays off. You end up paying the price with your health, relationships and reputation.

Karen Brody, CEO of Bold Tranquility and Bold Birth, recalls the breakthrough moment when she realised perfectionism coupled with an unhealthy determination to push through anything that was causing her to burnout:

Have you ever been all ready to go big and bold and find that real life slams you in the face? I sure have. Major flashback – Two kids. One with croup, one throwing up. Husband traveling in Africa. Work deadline. It's like one day you've got it all together...the sunshine is shining just about everywhere in your life...the kids are healthy...you're drinking that favorite tea...feeling surprisingly energetic...and the next minute life becomes this 'Little Engine That Could' movie that's gone all wrong.

I think I can, I think I can....I know I...CAN'T.

Can't? 'Can't' was never in my vocabulary. Until the past few years when I realized that can't is just as a strong and bold a word as can.

I've said a lot of cants in my business this year... Doing reality checks is one way I'm learning to keep it real around here.

Illusion of Urgency

In recent years we have become bombarded with multimedia messaging. From the moment we get woken by our radio alarm clocks, pick up the newspaper, turn on breakfast television or glance at our phones in the morning our brain starts uploading and processing new information.

The alerts we receive are designed to be attention grabbing and create an illusion of urgency, whether it is a 'breaking news' broadcast, a time-sensitive status update or the announcement of a sale that 'ends today!'.

Every time we find ourselves compulsively checking the media, we are exposing ourselves to more and more information. Feeling like we 'need to know' what is going on around us can become an addiction and distract us when we feel bored, restless or anxious. Like a nosey neighbor constantly peering out the window to see what Mr Jones is up to, we can feel compelled to stay on top of our e-mail and the latest news feeds, whether political, health, sports or general social networks.

This behaviour can lead to an information overload, which clogs our cognitive processing capacity and limits our ability to make decisions.[56] It can also rupture our relationships because it breaks the flow of conversations and diverts us from enjoying quality time with each other.

A study conducted by Nielsen Co. in 2012[57] found that 67% of Americans watch television while eating dinner. Technology company Techcrunch carried out a study[58] the same year, which found that 38% of Americans check e-mail whilst eating their evening meal.

Figures for the UK are similar. According to the *December 2010 TV Licensing's TeleScope Report*[59] 72% of us eat a main meal in front of the television (although this figure is slightly lower at 59% for those with children). With regard to checking emails, a 2012 study by *Good*[60] revealed that 29% of Brits scan their inbox during dinner.

When I was young, meal times were 'family time' and my mother would always urge us to switch the television off and communicate with each other. I believe she taught my brothers and me something very valuable in encouraging us to do that. It is a practice I continue to this day.

In the ten years that my husband and I have been together we have made an effort, whenever possible, to sit down each evening without distractions of phones, computers or the television when we eat. I believe it to be one of the keys to a happy marriage and for raising contented children.

In the spring of 2013 I was invited to appear on a UK current affairs chat show broadcast on SKY TV called the *Chrissy B Show*.[61] After the show I was intrigued to learn that the presenter, Christoulla Boodram, completed a 21-day media fast in order to help her become more aware of how television, web surfing and social media robbed her of her ability to concentrate on more important things. Recounting her experience of fasting in this way, Boodram said:

I didn't watch television for three weeks. I wasn't tweeting or searching online for things, unless it was work related. I noticed how many things had previously been taking away my attention. It helped me to reflect on myself and look deep inside.

How does multimedia messaging currently consume your attention?

Although it is difficult to avoid big advertising billboards in the street or radio in the shops, it is possible to make a conscious choice to cut down on the amount of media that you expose yourself to.

Do you find yourself checking your phone first thing in the morning and last thing at night?

What could you do to help break the addiction?

Switching off your Smartphone at meal times is a good place to start. Also consider a cut off time in the evening at least an hour before you go to bed to help you disconnect from your day and unwind ready for a good night's rest. Rather than taking your phone to bed with you, buy a silent alarm clock for your bedroom and leave your mobile in another room until the morning.

In a 2011 study conducted by Ofcom[62] the vast majority of Smartphone users (81%) admitted to having their mobiles switched on all of the time, even when they were in bed. Not only does this mean an increased temptation to check for news updates, email and social media status before attempting to go to sleep, making it extremely difficult for the mind to switch off from thinking, but you are more likely to get disturbed during the night too. The same Ofcom survey found that 38% of Smartphone users get woken by their phone whilst sleeping and respond to incoming calls, texts and other messages, rather than turning their device off.

What are some of the other daily habits you could change?

You may find it helpful to have a conversation with your partner and/or children and get them on board, too, so that you can encourage each other to become less dependent on needing to know what is going on in the world 24/7 and more dedicated to knowing what is going on with each other.

Making a change like this can bring up feelings of awkwardness and anxiety, partly because of the fear that by being cut off from the news, you somehow lose competitive advantage, which is an illusion because most news flashes are trivial and offer no real value. It is a common misconception that news consumption improves our decision-making. The fact is that relevant facts are overlooked by dramatic details that help to sell stories.

News leads us to walk around with the completely wrong risk maps in our heads. So terrorism is over-rated. Chronic stress is under-rated. The collapse of Lehman Brothers is over-rated. Fiscal irresponsibility is under-rated. Astronauts are over-rated. Nurses are under-rated.
Rolf Dobelli[63]

Cutting down on media consumption can also make us feel uncomfortable because in the moments when we used to rely on it to distract us from sitting with our feelings or avoid communication with others, we suddenly have nowhere to hide. But, if you are willing to sit with the discomfort for a while you will soon discover how to reconnect with yourself and others in far more natural and healthy ways.

John Donahoe, eBay CEO, makes a conscious choice to disconnect completely from multimedia during their annual family holiday. He believes that this time out to unplug is vital to help him recharge and be an effective leader:

> *This summer, I'll be heading to the same Cape Cod beach house I've been staying at with my family for the past 28 years. My kids hate the house for the same reason I love it: it has a rotary phone, the cell phone service stinks, and the closest Internet hub is two miles away at the local library.*

Try disconnecting for at least an hour each day and for extended periods of time at the weekends and holidays.

At times when you are alone and feel compelled to resume old habits of compulsive media checking, grab a pen and paper and write down whatever is on your mind instead. Allow yourself to write *anything* and everything. Nobody else needs to see what you write. At first you may write line after line of total dross, perhaps even page after page. That is okay. Keep writing.

The logical part of your brain is likely to want to analyse and criticise whatever you write. That is normal. As you continue to write in this way you will find that analytical thinking gradually begins to subside, allowing the creative part of your brain to engage.

Your creative brain is the connection to an inner power source that transcends the logical mind and shares flashes of inspiration, insight and wisdom. As children we instinctively knew how to be creative. Despite being born to indulge in being creative, as we grew up we gradually became accustomed to more 'adult' ways of doing things and began to forget how much fun it can be to do things for the sake of it, for the sake of having fun! Much of this is because we stopped being encouraged to take risks.

In deciding to consciously disconnect from multimedia you take a risk because you choose to live in the moment and return to a natural state of *being*. Spontaneously writing or drawing, instead of surfing the web, updating Facebook or scanning the news enables you to indulge your creativity and gives you an outlet for self-expression and exploration. Other creative activities like singing, dancing, painting, drumming or playing can also facilitate this.

If you want to return to the state of creativity that you accessed naturally as a child, you have to be bold, let your hair down, give yourself permission to be silly and remember how to play.

What do you remember doing as a child? Perhaps crafting castles, playing with your dog, building Lego fortresses, dressing up as a fairy princess or jumping around on a pogo stick?

To reconnect with your inner child and rediscover your ability to play, schedule an afternoon off and have fun with some of the following:

- Get messy with finger painting.
- Pop on some wellies and splash in a muddy puddle.
- Build a den in the forest.
- Pretend to be a superhero/heroine and fly around the room as if you were the strongest, fastest, bravest person on the planet.
- Grab an assortment of pots and pans from your kitchen cupboards and create your own band.
- Buy yourself an adult-sized space hoppers and have fun bouncing around the garden.

If it has been a while since you have talked with your partner or family during dinner, then a helpful mealtime conversation starter is to ask each person around the table to take turns sharing the best thing that happened to them during the course of the day. This is an especially useful practice to instill in children, because in order to find their favourite memory, they naturally think through each stage of their day so that they can recall the moment that made them smile the most. In doing this they develop several skills, including the ability to look for silver linings. As adults it does us no harm to work on this too!

As a result of cutting down on media not only will your relationships improve, but you are also likely to find that you generally feel happier because you are no longer being constantly assaulted by negative stories in the news. As the saying goes 'no news is good news'. Our society has become hooked on bad press.

> *The media feeds us small bites of trivial matter, tidbits that don't really concern our lives and don't require thinking... we are beginning to realise how toxic news can be.*
> Rolf Dolbelli

Interrupting

In our rush to fit more into every area of our lives, including our conversations, we stop listening and do things like finish off each other's sentences, paraphrase each other's words, moan, interrupt, get irritated, give advice, jump in to try to solve each other's problems or allow ourselves to get distracted. As a result our conversations are hurried and fragmented.

> *Most people are aware that other people don't listen, but they are not nearly as aware that they themselves don't listen.*
> Mary Siegel

One of the most powerful things you can do for yourself, your partner, your friends, colleagues and children is simply to listen.

It is not until we listen to ourselves that we can really listen to others. This is because truly listening requires the listener to be in a state of ease, focused only on the moment and on what the other person has to say.

Nancy Kline, Founder and President of Time to Think, suggests that when we give another person the gift of our undivided attention, listen to them with ease and stay fully present in the moment shared with them, something truly profound happens – we create a space for them that determines the quality of their thinking. The creation of this kind of thinking space enables clarity of thought, eloquence of speech, and the generation of ideas:

Most people think they listen well, but they rarely do... Ease creates. Urgency destroys. When it comes to helping people think for themselves, sometimes doing means not doing.

When we truly learn to listen for ourselves and for others, we free ourselves to pay attention without urgency, enjoy the uniqueness of being in the moment, encourage with authenticity, create trust and mutual respect, and foster dreams that unfold with ease. Listening in this way has the power to transform your relationship with yourself, at home and with those at work. Listening has the power to transform our societies and the world we live in.

Until recent years much of our conditioning has emphasised the importance of appearing to be strong and have all the answers, belittling others in order to gain superiority, valuing competition and control, encouraging weakness to be covered up with lies. We were taught to sublimate our individuality and focus on conquering instead of collaborating.

These archaic models of relating are thankfully beginning to crumble. Organisations are realising the benefits of opening and encouraging diversity, appreciating individual qualities and characteristics, operating with honesty and integrity, establishing equality, asking questions about what is most needed and most importantly, *listening*.

We may still have far to go, but we can each start today in our own way by beginning to listen more to ourselves and to the people in our lives and by recognising the potential genius within everyone we meet.

If we treat a man as he is, we make him less than he is. If we treat a man as though he already were what he potentially could be, we make him what he should be.
Goethe

Top Tips to Improve Your Listening

1. **Begin by listening to yourself** and honoring your needs. Give yourself what you need. Nourish and nurture yourself. Create an environment for yourself that says 'you matter'. In doing these things for yourself, you permit others to do the same for themselves. By truly valuing yourself, you automatically start valuing others. Your interactions with others will also improve as a result.

   In listening to your own feelings and acknowledging them, you will find it easier to acknowledge the feelings of others. Allow other people to release their emotions in your presence. Thinking can be restored when given the space for sufficient emotional release.

   When someone verbally expresses a feeling to you – like anger, fear, sadness or joy – reflect back to them that you have acknowledged it (e.g., 'sounds like you're angry about x' or 'looks like you are really excited about y').

   As humans, we all seek to receive love and acknowledgement from others. Remind others that they can be sure of you and that you are there for them:

Piglet sidled up to Pooh from behind. 'Pooh,' he whispered.'Yes, Piglet?''Nothing,' said Piglet, taking Pooh's paw, 'I just wanted to be sure of you.'
A. A. Milne

2. **Relax into your conversations with others**. Let go of any sense of rush. Stay gently focused on the moment and give your undivided attention to what the other person has to say. In doing this you will find that the other person is more clearly and concisely able to state what they want to say.

3. **Treat others as your equal**, regardless of hierarchy and even with children. This improves the quality of the attention you are able to give to the other person and fosters respect and intelligibility so that any tendency towards infantalisation or assumed superiority is removed.

4. **Give people a chance.** Rather than jumping in to give someone your advice or trying to solve their 'problems', give people a chance to find their own solutions. Ask them questions to help them think. Encourage them to think for themselves.

5. **Foster hope.** Permit yourself to become fascinated by what others have to say. Don't interrupt or humiliate. Allow people to share their true thoughts and feelings with you without cynicism. Respect their dreams. Encourage them to dream.

6. **Give genuine praise.**Tell people the things you like about them, their ideas, their work – if you are giving constructive feedback to someone apply a 5:1 ratio of positive-to-negative criticism. Allow the one area for improvement to be the thing that, if improved, would positively affect everything else. People think more creatively in a context of genuine praise.

7. **Be open and honest**, with yourself and with others. This will improve your ability to listen and to overcome challenges. Often facing something you've been denying can unblock stifled energy and lead to creative genius.

Fear of Change

Whenever I start working with a new client I ask: 'How would you benefit if nothing was to change?'

At first people usually appear surprised by this question and state that they are determined to change and that the cost of things staying the same or getting worse far outweigh any benefits.

While it is great to identify what is at risk if nothing changes, because this often provides motivation to change, it is equally important to explore the benefits of doing nothing. The reason for doing this is for you to check whether there might be a hidden part of you that fears change. Hidden fear can sabotage success. But, when we shine a light on our fears we often discover they are trying to protect us and simply require some reassurance in order to release their hold.

I have created the following art exercise to help you identify, acknowledge and move through your fears.

Feel Your Fear Exercise

1. First Self-Portrait – False Image

In order connect with this inner part of yourself it can be helpful to first shed the false image that you have been striving to maintain – the 'you' that others have come to expect so much from, the 'you' that has constantly been under pressure to deliver and prove competent in any given scenario.

Grab a pen or pastels and a pad of paper and draw a self-portrait of the person you show to the world. You may wish to write around it any of the qualities that you have struggled to exhibit, the things you are admired for, the tasks you perform, your various roles, the expectations others have of you and those you have of yourself.

2. Shake

Put your self-portrait aside. Stand up and physically shake your body with the intention of releasing the draining energy of this false image and allowing the other you to reveal him/herself.

3. Close Your Eyes

Allow the other you to emerge. Use all of your senses to *hear* the other you speak. You may gradually begin to notice inner whisperings, feel subtle sensations, experience faint imagery in your mind's eye or gain a sense of inner knowing dropping into your consciousness. Allow the information to come to you in whatever form it takes.

4. Second Self-Portrait – Other You

Draw a second portrait of you now. An image that represents the part of you that you experience when you first wake in the morning. Add the words of the voice that speaks to you when you are alone and forcing yourself to struggle on.

5. Questions

Ask this other part of yourself what it wants you to know. Write the response(s) you receive to the following questions in the first person:

What am I afraid of if things change?

- Am I afraid of upsetting someone?
- Am I afraid of letting someone down?
- Am I afraid of getting too big?
- Am I afraid of losing control?

- Am I afraid of failing?
- Am I afraid of something else?
- What do I need to recognise in order to move forward?

To foster and grow our confidence so that we can move beyond burnout and live our lives connected with our inner brilliance, we need to take aligned action, move through our fears and be brave enough to show up as a more authentic version of ourselves in the world.

Many of us do not feel confident expressing ourselves authentically in certain situations because we allow negative, self-limiting thoughts to prevent us from staying connected to our true self. Rather than acknowledging our fears and actually allowing ourselves to feel them, we try to push the fears down, ignore them or cut them off; this causes frustration, resentment and disconnection from our inner self. By trying to ignore our fears we stop ourselves from facing them and moving through them.

Many of us carry confidence-crushing beliefs from childhood that prevent us taking action on doing the things we would really love to do. Just as we are about to begin something that takes us out of our comfort zone, in pops the little voice in our head saying, 'you won't make it', 'you're not good enough', 'who do you think you are, or 'get back in your box!'. That voice can lead to feelings of fear and stop us from taking the very action required to bring about the result we long for.

If we engage with our fear, rather than cutting it off, then we can communicate with it and discover why it is presenting itself – find out what purpose it is trying to serve us.

Usually fear arises to try to protect us from an envisaged negative outcome like rejection, humiliation or the inability to cope. Often it kicks in somewhat prematurely, when we start focusing on the worst-case scenario, preventing us from looking at the bigger picture and checking out how bad the worst thing that could happen really is. When we suppress our fears we get trapped in a negative cycle. This can lead to feelings of regret, disappointment or worthlessness.

By interacting with our fear we can allow the energy that it brings to flow through us. We can literally discharge the fear through our bodies. The next time you notice fear rising up within you, rather than fighting that feeling, I invite you to take a deep breath and really feel it. Notice it. Exaggerate it.

Make any involuntary movement in your body a bit bigger. Act out the butterflies in your tummy. Draw a picture of your fear. Write a poem about it. Sing to it. Talk to the part of you feeling the fear. Experiment, get creative and play with it. If you are with other people and not able to engage with your fears alone, try talking about the fears openly with others. Gently acknowledge your fears in conversation. Use humour. Be willing to have fun with your fears.

Do whatever feels right for you. Use your fear. Before long you will probably notice that it has discharged, and you no longer feel it.

You block your dream when you allow your fear to grow bigger than your faith.
Mary Manin Morrissey

You can and will overcome burnout. Reassure your fear that you will now focus on prioritising self-care. Focus on the positive results you are capable of creating in your life. In doing this you reconnect with inner desires that represent the essence of who you are. Fear subsides because it cannot coexist in that space.

In the film *After Earth*, the character General Cypher Rage, played by actor Will Smith, turns to his son and says:

Fear is not real. The only place that fear can exist is in our thoughts of the future. It is a product of our imagination, causing us to fear things that do not at present and may not ever exist... Fear is a choice.

Whenever you feel fear, allow yourself to acknowledge it, mobilise it and move through it; then encourage yourself with positive thoughts and affirmations like 'it's ok', 'you can do this', 'go for it', 'you'll be alright'.

Busyness

When you awoke this morning, what was the first thing on your mind? On your list of Things To Do, what is number one? As you contemplate your current priorities, is there a person at the top, or is it some kind of doingness?

Neale Donald Walsch

I used to be addicted to busyness. I could not sit still for longer than five minutes without feeling the urgent need to be doing something productive. There was always something drawing my attention that needed 'doing'. I was unaware that I had made busyness the purpose of my life. In all of my busyness I forgot to look after myself.

It was not until I burnt out that I was forced to do nothing. My battery was so flat that no matter how much I wanted to be doing something, I simply couldn't. When I surrendered to giving my body the rest it so desperately needed I discovered the precious gift of allowing myself to be still. I learned that being still is incredibly powerful. In being still I could finally feel my body communicating with me. As I took the time to listen I found that I had access to a sense of inner understanding and a level of intuition that I never previously knew existed – the same deep well of wisdom and voice of guidance that resides within us all and connects us with each other.

If, like me you have spent what seems like your whole life being busy, then practicing being still can be extremely challenging. Even now, I need to remind myself to take time to be still; otherwise old busyness habits will try to creep back in.

The purpose of your life is not to be as busy as possible... Being busy can be purposeful and productive, but when you are permanently busy, it is a sure sign that your busyness conceals a lack of clarity, a fear of inadequacy, feelings of unworthiness, and a lack of faith in your soul's ability to help you live your purpose.

Dr Robert Holden

Chinese philosopher, Lao Tzu once said, 'When nothing is done, nothing is left undone.' This used to completely bemuse me, but what I notice time and time again if I start to feel myself tapering towards overscheduling, overcommitting or overextending myself, is that if I purposefully lessen my load and give myself permission to do nothing, more miraculously ends up getting done.

My favorite 15-minute break is to lay down flat on my back and do nothing... Sometimes I spend my 15 minutes focusing on all the things I have to be grateful for, and sometimes I try to clear my mind and meditate. Any of these allow me to get up after 15 minutes feeling refreshed and reenergized.

Donna Skeels Cygan, financial planner

Experiment with inviting silence into your life. Give yourself permission to be still and do nothing when you feel most inclined to resist taking rest. Silence can be a powerful tool to help combat busyness. It assists us in hearing our inner voice and connects us with our inner resources.

Need-to-Know Summary
- When we burnout our energy becomes severely depleted.
- Energy management techniques can help us to protect, support, replenish, and renew our energy.
- An essential key to recovery from burnout is the prioriti-

sation of regaining energy, health and well-being via a practice of extreme self-care.

- We must first take care of ourselves before we can take care of others.
- It is helpful to use the *Balance Wheel Exercise* featured in this chapter to take stock on each area of your life and identify what you most want to change.
- You are what you eat. Exhausted adrenals need replenishment with a combination of rest, good nutrition and gentle, graduated exercise.
- Sleep is critical for rebuilding the body and recovering from burnout.
- Time is the most valuable asset you have. It is important to honour and protect it by letting go of old commitments and learning to say 'no'.
- You can reclaim your power by deciding to view the things that you used to tolerate in your life from a different vantage point, practising forgiveness and taking a 'zero tolerance' approach.
- Energetic preservation and defence is equally as important as physical preservation and defence.
- Energy protection techniques, like the martial arts-inspired *Protection Process* featured in this chapter, can help us minimise the weakening effect of external influences on our energy.
- In order to improve the results we experience in any area of our lives we need to improve our thinking, self-talk and the statements we regularly use.
- Sometimes we need to completely disconnect from people and commitments in our lives that have been excessively depleting us or that no longer inspire us.
- People and places both from our past and present can drain us. Even when a relationship with someone has ended, we have moved homes or changed jobs, we can still feel

energetically exhausted if we have not cleared residual electro-magnetic energy attachments.

- The *Cord Cutting Method* featured in this chapter is a simple visualisation process that can be used to disconnect from negative attachments, beliefs and energy sources using the power of your intention.
- Whenever we process and release old beliefs and feelings, and consciously replace them with more positive, empowering ones, we cause neuroplastic changes in the brain, influencing all of our internal organs and their connecting systems.
- By changing your thoughts, you change your health and your life.
- Meditation is an excellent burnout prevention and recovery tool.
- The *Burnout Root Cause Meditation* featured in this chapter is designed to find and heal the root cause belief that has ultimately resulted in your experience of burnout.
- While rapid recovery is completely possible, it is important to follow your intuition with your recovery and not push yourself to do too much too soon.
- The *Power Shout* technique featured in this chapter can help you reconnect with your inner power and regain confidence to lovingly assert yourself in various situations.
- It is possible for both men and women to 'have it all', but we need to find flexibility in the way we work in order to achieve this.
- Perfectionism contributes to burnout. Wherever possible practice patience instead of perfectionism.
- Switch off your Smartphone and disconnect from other sources of multi media messaging to help overcome the illusion of urgency.
- Learn to listen – to yourself *and* others. Listening has the power to transform our societies and the world we live in.

- Fear is not real. Whenever you feel fear allow yourself to acknowledge it, mobilise it and move through it; then encourage yourself with positive thoughts and affirmations.
- Challenge your busyness by being still.

Table 2.1: Commitment Exercise

Life Area	Commitments	Enthusiasm
Work		
Family		
Money		
Spirituality		
Love & Romance		
Home		
Creativity		
Health and Fitness		
Rest and Relaxation		
Friends and Social Life		

PART 3 – BRILLIANCE

Writing a New Script

Although no one can go back and make a brand-new start, anyone can start from now and make a brand-new ending.
Carl Bard

Early into this book I described the diamond of true brilliance that you hold within. All of the exercises that I have given you so far will have helped you to clear anything keeping your brilliance hidden and preventing you from connecting to the abundant power and potential you hold within.

The next exercise will help you call forth the essence of your inner diamond by inviting you to get creative. This exercise was introduced to me during my postgraduate degree training in integrative art psychotherapy. I have used it with hundreds of clients to help them uncover their brilliance.

Mask of Potential

Masks have been used since ancient times for ceremony, story-telling, entertainment, disguise and protection. It is often said that we wear metaphoric masks in different scenarios to help us play the various parts of ourselves, bring forth different skills and talents and reveal certain strengths. A similar comparison is also made to hats being 'worn' in the different roles we play in our everyday lives.

The creative act of making a mask can serve as a potent tool for awareness, self-exploration and change. Being creative connects us with the self's natural universal energy, *physis* – the healthy inner core that enables change. Art can help facilitate a healing process of becoming aware, accepting and letting go of previous identities in order to rediscover, and re-birth, our true self.

Creativity is the natural order of life. Life is energy: pure creative energy. There is an underlying, in-dwelling creative force infusing all of life – including ourselves. When we open ourselves to our creativity, we open ourselves up to the creator's creativity within us and our lives. We are, ourselves, creations. And we, in turn, are meant to continue creativity by being creative ourselves.

Julia Cameron

In transforming your life from burnout to brilliance you are moving through a creative process of releasing the old to recreate yourself anew and discover how to more authentically express your true self.

By being yourself, you put something wonderful in the world that was not there before.

Edwin Elliot

The process of making your own mask can be used to help you explore the part of yourself that you have most likely concealed from the world, the part that holds your true potential and inner brilliance.

Many people become creatively blocked when they allow their fear of judgment from others to prevent them from enjoying their natural artistic instincts. For best results, give your inner critic the day off. Allow your inner child the freedom to get messy and give yourself permission to get as creative as you like.

Give him a mask and he will tell you the truth.

Oscar Wilde

To make a quick and easy mask, go to the book website, www.jaynemorris.com, where you will find a mask template sheet that you can print off, cut out and stick onto a piece of card. All you need to do next is decorate the mask with your choice of crayons, paints, pastels, feathers, gems, glitter, leaves, stickers and anything else you feel drawn to. Finish by fixing a couple of ribbons or some string on either side of the mask so that it can be securely tied to your head.

Once you have created your mask, sit alone with a mirror and ask the person you see in the reflection the following questions, or ask someone you trust to read them to you and to write down the answers that emerge. When answering, start each sentence in the first person – e.g., 'I ...'

- Who are you?
- What supports your growth/existence?
- What do you long for?
- What do you need to change in your life to flourish and fly?
- If you could do anything what would you do?
- If you could create anything what would you create?
- If you could be more fully connected to your true brilliance how would this impact your life?
- Is there a way for your body to convey something of your essence?
- Who are you here to be?

Art Experiments

It is only in being creative, that the individual discovers the self.
Donald Winnicott

I encourage you to experiment with art to help you discover more about yourself and how to stay aligned with your brilliance. Creativity can take any shape or form, for true creativity is any expression of being alive.

We experience the world through all of our senses, and the psyche therefore processes our feelings and emotions visually, audibly and kinaesthetically.

Give yourself the opportunity to explore your emotional experiences using various art forms – drawing, painting, clay, puppetry, creative writing, journaling, poetry, music, dance, storytelling and play. Doing so will help you to externalise and communicate inner pictures, dialogues, energies and atmospheres with greater access to your sensory expression.

As a result you will naturally become increasingly self-aware and therefore more able to identify any unhealthy patterns of relating.

By becoming aware we gain important information about our past, thus providing a 'road map' for ways to facilitate change in our life ahead.

There are a few further art exercises included in the next section that involve poetry, storytelling, drama and vision boards. I have found them to be especially powerful in helping my clients access greater levels of creativity and inspiration in order to find new ways of moving forward and clarifying the details of a road map for the future. Do take the time to try them; this kind of work may seem light on the surface, but it penetrates the emotions at a very deep level.

For people to be able to organize their lives, they must have access to their emotions.
Alice Miller

Poetry Exercise

Poetry is made by belief. It thinks and speaks in imagery. Its thought body can take you into uninhabited realms; the unthinkable becomes visible and makes you think about the invisible.
Margo Fuchs, Foundations of Expressive Arts Therapies (Stephen Levine)

Poetry enables us to go within, connect with our inner guidance, uncover and challenge limiting beliefs and reconnect to inspiration and inner brilliance. It can be a powerful tool for self-expression, exploration and transformation.

I once facilitated a transpersonal coaching seminar in which I explored the benefits of art exercises with participants. Poetry particularly resonated with a student named Sue Maggot. At first Sue admitted that she was not really interested in attempting to write poetry at all and was quite apprehensive about it. Yet, once she gave it a try she found that it 'sparked an almost strange, emotional connection' and 'seemed to touch some untapped creativity and unexpressed emotion buried deep inside'.

After the course Sue felt so inspired by the experience that she set up a business specialising in the use of poetry to create powerful connections for profitable businesses. Sue started writing poetry to capture the essence of events she attended and wrote poems commissioned by others. She published a poetry anthology in 2012 entitled *Believe! The Gift of Inspiration for Female Entrepreneurs* and was short-listed for a national Women Inspiring Women award that summer.

If you notice resistance towards attempting some of the exercises in this book, be reassured that is normal – give them a go anyway, because what you might uncover as a result might truly astound you.

To ease you into the process of writing poetry, first try to write a simple three line poem. One word, then two words, then one word. Here is an example:

Burnout
Exhausted life
Healed

Now build on this a little further. Throw away the rulebook. Your poem does not need to rhyme; it can be any shape or length. See what flows when you set yourself a title, for example 'My

Essence':

My Essence

Is brilliance
It is shining, it is bright
It is the guidance from within
That comes when I need it
Day or night

When I feel stuck
Or blocked by fear
I ask it what I can do
And the wisdom comes
Inspiring and clear

My essence
Wants me to share
The unique qualities I have
It helps me to be radiant
In everything I do

My essence
Helps me recognise
When to rest and when to give
It helps me find a balance
In the way I live.

Once your creative juices are really flowing, experiment with creating a freestyle poem, like this fantastic piece written by Sue:

Believe!

Sue, stand up, stand up! Be bold, be strong!
Your talent, on world stage, truly does belong!

You are a beacon, shining bright,
Birthed to emerge, grow, and shine your inner light!

It is a crime to leave talent, dusty on a rickety, hidden shelf,
Set out your stall; allow true expression of your amazing inner self.
Surely, you will experience some discomfort as you stretch,
Far better than staying a self-defeating, self-pitying little wretch?
Rather, as you experience movement, create life-changing shifts,
You will, newly emboldened, dare to share your gifts!

Life is truly meant for us to live; by our own example, give
To those, like us, who have sometimes been
Squashed, ignored, or diligently working; self-effacing, behind a
   screen
Of uniformity; water poured on burning fire,
Quashed down, made damp squib of all passion and desire.

And, as others bask in your new golden glow,
It helps for them, also to know,
That they have their own miracles to perform,
Whether on a stage, or as more often is the norm,
In their own families and communities, through their daily life and
   deeds,
Do great work; sow and nurture the seeds
Of positivity, purposefulness and joy,
With which we all entered this world to buoy
Up ourselves and others, manifest the birth right of our mothers,
As we mix with friends, many others, who enter into our life's
   stratosphere.
All add dark and shade, maybe cause us to shed a tear,
Perhaps of joy or sometimes pain,
So, ultimately, of our own truth, understanding we gain.

Right here and now, we need to show,

Through heartfelt determination, strength of courage,
We all have the power to foster our own abilities, to grow;
Achieve our birth right to succeed; root out the dreaded weed
That with stranglehold choked down our well intentioned schemes,
Left us struggling with dashed hopes, and broken, once beautiful
dreams.

So meaning-full, join us to create,
An interwoven, brilliant picture with which all can relate!
As one voice, stand up and state:

We are here to live mindfully in this life,
We choose creativity, positive intent over unrewarding strife
And as we choose to change how we ourselves perceive,
In our own dreams, our legacy, our power, we truly believe!

By Sue Maggott

Storytelling Exercise

This exercise uses storytelling to build on the previous exercises and help you shape a new script for your life. First imagine you are writing a character study for you new self. Begin by describing the following:

- What qualities do you have?
- How do you live your life?
- How do you make decisions?
- What are your priorities?
- How do you interact with others?
- What are the beliefs you hold about yourself?

Next, get up out of your chair and improvise acting out the part of your new character. Imagine yourself one year from now moving through your ideal day. Begin with how you get up in the morning:

- What are the first thoughts that your character has?
- What is his/her morning routine?
- How does he/she move his/her body out of the bed?
- How does the new you prepare for the day ahead?
- As you move through your day what are your interactions like with other people?
- What is your thinking like?
- How is your energy?
- How do you feel towards the end of the day?
- How do you spend your evenings?
- What do you choose to focus on before you go to bed?
- How do you feel when you go to sleep?

Rehearse a few scenarios from your ideal day. Next you may choose to write out your new script on paper. Alternatively you may wish to draw a picture or comic book-style cartoon strip or create a version of it as a song, an interpretative dance, a poem or simply reinforce it by acting other parts of it out like a play in your head.

Go with whatever feels the most inspiring and fun.

Infuse your script with affirming new thoughts and beliefs, reinforce the lessons and learnings that you want to carry with you into the future. Honour and celebrate all the things that have shaped your strengths and qualities by imagining you are collecting all of these things up inside of you. Allow them to reinforce the brilliance of your inner diamond. Feel your energy getting lighter and growing brighter as you move through this process.

Music

Music is within you, in the very beating of your heart. When you begin to notice rhythms of life you open yourself up to hearing music in every moment, in the silence of the night, in the singing of the birds, in the movements of every living thing.

We are constantly creating music as part of an incredible orchestra of life, each playing a part and dancing to the beat of our own drums. When we get caught up in the whirlwind of our day-to-day activities we don't hear this music. We override the rhythms of our body and stop listening. But we can reconnect with it at any time by simply tapping on the table with our fingers or popping in our headphones and selecting a track on our iPhone.

My idea is that there is music in the air, music all around us; the world is full of it, and you simply take as much as you require.
Edward Elgar

Indulging in your instinctive ability to create music can be hugely therapeutic and help you to get in touch and experience your emotions rather than suppressing them. Music can also help facilitate healing and can be used to help you relax and re-energise when recovering from burnout.

Music has been used for healing for thousands of years across the globe, but the world of modern medicine is only just beginning to understand the complexity of its benefits.

In a BBC series about the power of music,[64] Jane Hansen detailed how recent medical research has resulted in the introduction of specially designed music programmes in 8,000 US hospitals, which are helping shorten the length of stay for premature babies by up to 12 days. The series also explains how research findings indicate that tailor made music programmes are enabling reductions in drug dosage requirements of patients by up to 50% and alleviating pain of certain unpleasant medical procedures.

I recommend listening to joyful music as part of an overall prescription for maintaining good health.
Dr Michael Miller

Science is starting to explain how music affects our brainwaves and organs in our body, alters our state of consciousness and creates changes in our neurons and blood-carrying cells. Music has been proven to have the power to regulate the heart, boost hormones, relax and deepen our breathing, lower blood pressure, release endorphins and increase blood flow. If certain music is played with a slow, rhythmic beat the heart will actually adapt to the beat of the music, which can be extremely beneficial for people suffering with conditions caused by stress and anxiety.

Some of the greatness of music however, lies in its holistic nature that all the elements form a unique wholeness, which may not be understood by studying the parts separately. However complex, music is readily appreciated by the mind without the need for formal knowledge.
Bombay Jayashri Ramnath

We might not yet understand fully how music actually heals, or even have scratched the surface of its full potential, but perhaps we do not need to know – we just need to trust that it works by some miracle larger than ourselves.

By tuning into our body and our emotions we can choose the music our body needs to help it operate optimally. The key is listening to what you like and feel you need. There is no right or wrong; trust what feels right for you – you might fancy a bit of Beethoven one day, Marilyn Manson then next, or want to bang a drum one moment then switch to strumming a harp. Indulge in whatever resonates with how you feel.

When we allow ourselves to explore our emotions through music we enrich our lives and enable feelings to flow through us.

Take a music bath once or twice a week for a few seasons. You will find it is to the soul what a water bath is to the body.
Oliver Wendell Holmes

Six Simple Ways to Reconnect With Music:

1. **Wake up to music** that makes you feel good – set your alarm to your favourite tune or song, so that you are woken gently by music that eases you into the day, rather than the rude awakening of the traditional alarm.

2. **Connect with your uncomfortable emotions** – if you're feeling angry, sad, tired or lonely and find yourself wanting to override the emotion and ignore it – stop! Play some music that reflects your mood or find an instrument and experiment with expressing your emotion by making sounds (even if it's the homemade kind, like a pot and spoon). You can even do this with your voice. If you feel shy, sing or shout into a pillow. Engage with your feelings. Allow yourself to really feel them, embody them. Flow with whatever comes up for you. What is the emotion trying to tell you? What does it want you to know?

3. **Compliment your creativity** – We all experience 'writers block' in some form or another from time to time; when we struggle to come up with an idea for an activity to do with our kids at the weekend, what to make for dinner, what colour we want to paint the kitchen or how to put together the report we're writing at work. By playing music that makes us feel inspired and allowing ourselves to be fully present in the moment, we can free up our creativity and connect back in with our inner genius. Before we know it we've discovered a great idea, and another, and another.

Music is the wine, which inspires one to new generative processes, and I am Bacchus who presses out this glorious wine for mankind

and makes them spiritually drunken.
Ludwig van Beethoven

4. **Lift your mood with your favourite song** – when faced with a chore like the washing up or laundry, or finding yourself putting off getting started on a project, pop on your favourite track and allow yourself to fully engage with the music. Stay in the present moment with the music, feel it flow through your body. If possible sing along, dance along and really enjoy it. Before you know it you'll be ready to get into whatever you've been putting off and might even find you have fun doing it!

5. **Release stress** – find some music that helps you relax and keep it handy at work, at home, on your phone or iPod and in the car. Whenever you feel tension building in your body, notice it and take a moment to listen to what message it has for you. Indulge in your relaxation music and use it to help you let go of stress. Imagine your body melting like butter while the music washes over you and allow it to take all your stress away. This is particularly useful when you are stuck in traffic or find yourself experiencing road rage after a frustrating encounter with another driver.

6. **Prepare for success** – if you are about to go into an important meeting, pitch an idea to your boss, run a race or face another type of challenge get your mind set for success by playing a motivating track that you associate with success. Boxers do this before big fights to get them in the right frame of mind to take on their opponent. Find a song that gets you up and has you raring to go – you might surprise yourself at what a powerful effect this can have.

Mapping Out Your Future

This chapter will focus on providing you with tools and techniques to map out and design the future you now want to live.

Expressing Gratitude

Before moving clients forward I like to invite them first to connect with the power of gratitude to help raise their awareness of the good things already in their lives.

> *I am endlessly grateful. Every day I'm grateful... How in the world I was born in this time to my parents in this world, right, as opposed to another time, a slum in India -I am so grateful. I'm grateful for everything.... I got grateful when I got fired. I said, 'How many people get to be fired and it's on the front page of the Wall Street Journal?'*
> Sallie Krawcheck, former president of the Global Wealth & Investment Management division of Bank of America

Expressing gratitude in our lives is something we can so easily forget to do, especially whenever our focus gets stuck on what is going wrong, rather than appreciating what is going right. It is so easy to get caught up in daily struggles and forget the countless blessings all around us.

I have always loved the concept of the American Thanksgiving, traditionally celebrated every November to give thanks for the autumn harvest, now used to express gratitude in general. Families and friends gather together to take time out from their busy lives and give thanks for all the wonder they experience, including the love they share with each other.

When was the last time you stopped for a moment to smile and behold the beauty in your life?

As the saying goes: 'You get what you focus on." When you

focus more on the good than the bad, you receive more of it! And vice versa. This is because whatever we think about effects how we feel in our body and determines the actions we take. Our thoughts also effect our energetic vibration, attracting to us the people, places, opportunities and things aligned with our energy. We are literally like magnets drawing towards us whatever we focus our attention on.

Every day... I choose to be in an attitude of gratitude. I get to choose how each day begins and receive the positive energy that accompanies my awareness and gratitude for all the many blessings in my life... Gratitude may not be the greatest of virtues,but it is the parent of all the others.
Lee Brower

Shifting our thoughts so that we regularly notice and express thanks for the things we are grateful for in our lives can be referred to as switching to a gratitude attitude. Like forming any new habit, this can at first take a little effort and perseverance, but within as little as 21 days, it is likely to have already become second nature.

One of the oldest traditions linked to gratitude is the act of giving thanks or 'saying grace' before and/ or after eating a meal. Whenever introducing something new into your daily routine it is often easiest to tie it in with another regular practice – eating is a good one!

After spending three years living and working in Japan I became so accustomed to the Japanese tradition of expressing gratitude before and after meals that I automatically continued the practice when I returned to the UK.

In many other countries it is also customary to express gratitude by saying a prayer or express an unvoiced intention at mealtimes, the act of which tends to be rooted in a religion like Christianity, Judaism, Baha'i, Islam and Hinduism.

You do not need to follow a religion to give thanks before eating. Use your mealtimes to quiet your mind for a moment and turn your attention towards all the things you are grateful for in your life. An easy one to get you started is to be thankful for having food to eat. Then turn your attention to yourself. Often self-admiration can be viewed in our society as selfish, but self-gratitude in this sense of the term is about appreciating that you are an absolutely amazing human being, right now in this moment.

Be thankful for the miracle of your every breath, your very being. Express thanks for all the things that make you so uniquely you. Notice how good it feels in your body to spend some time focusing on positive thoughts.

Develop an attitude of gratitude starting with you – you are worth it! Take a moment right now and look at yourself – your hands, your feet, and your face – with the same kind of admiration you might bestow on one of the most precious sculptures in the Louvre Museum in Paris. Think about this: you are irreplaceable, which makes you priceless!

Joyce Schwartz

Gratitude List

Think of the things, places and people in your life that you are thankful for and make a list of 10 things you are happy to have in your life.

You can always add to this list. An easy way to expand your list is to run through the alphabet and for each letter a – z, fill in the name of something or someone you are grateful for.

Gratitude can also help to powerfully shift your view of burnout from that of a curse to a blessing:

Burnout signals not despair but hope. Recognized and attended to, it can become a positive energy force, signifying that the time has come for a cease and desist action, a hard look at yourself, and a

change to something new.
Dr Herbert Freudenberger

When Jayne Fountain, CEO of The Fountain Institute, became so busy that she was brought to an abrupt halt with the experience of a heart attack, she realised that thankfulness had long been missing from her life. She experienced overwhelming gratitude one day when her neighbours came to her assistance and helped tend to her garden. She became determined to be a 'more caring, empathetic individual'. As she began to practice being thankful she discovered that 'even in the middle of great sorrow' this brought her joy:

> *Today my life overflows with thanksgiving for every day that I live, for every breath that I take, and for every person that I am privileged to meet.*

In developing thankfulness Jayne says:

> *I discovered that thankfulness develops strength within us... I had hidden the wonderful, loving, and kind person that I was on the inside, behind a mask of type A, high performance, high achieving, and highly controlling behaviors... After hours of crying, exhausted and empty, I thanked God for who I was. I acknowledged honestly my faults, my abilities, and my talents, and I expressed thankfulness for all of it!*

New Life, New Priorities

I don't want to be the richest man in the graveyard.
Charlie Mullins

When someone comes to me expressing concern that they are burning out, or wanting to recover from burnout, I often ask them to list their top five priorities. Then I ask them to list the five areas where they have been directing the majority of their energy and attention. Usually there is a mismatch between the two.

For example, you may list your family as your number one, but when you reflect upon whether your family would *feel* that they are your number-one priority you realise that you have unintentionally made other things more important in terms of where you devote your energy and time.

The things we spend most of our time pursuing turn out to be what we find least important.
Lolly Daskal

Work can often be used as an excuse for self-neglect and neglect of the things we truly care about.

When one of my clients experienced a breakthrough realisation around her priorities, it awakened her to the fact her self-neglect had been creating patterns of burnout not only for herself but also for her two boys.

Helen had built a multi-million pound business empire with her husband and pushed herself on many occasions to work harder and longer than her body could cope with. As a result of not giving her body the opportunity to recover from pneumonia she suffered from a serious respiratory problem and sought ongoing professional help and treatment in an attempt to repair the long-term damage.

When I asked her what her priorities were, she listed her health and her family as her main concerns. Yet, she also identified that these two areas were given the least of her energy and attention. She confessed that she often got so absorbed in her work that she would forget to eat. She worked such long hours that she never used her gym membership. Her reason for working so hard was that she wanted to be able to give her sons the best opportunities possible with their education and personal development.

Helen's elder son attended a top boarding school and was under significant pressure to stay at the top of his scholarship class. Whenever he returned home for visits at the weekend, their time together was limited because she had arranged several private tutoring sessions for him, on top of which he had a heavy load of homework.

Her younger son had a weekday schedule so full of extracurricular sessions and lessons after school that he fell asleep straight after dinner, and his nanny put him to bed. His weekends were equally busy with classes, activities and extra learning experiences.

Helen identified that not only was she getting to spend so little quality time with her sons, but that every time she cleared her schedule for a family vacation, she fell ill, and both her sons would get sick too. When she explored why this happened she realised it was because they all pushed so hard during term-time. When the holidays arrived they were all so tired from working so hard that their bodies shut down to physically make them take a break.

Helen shocked herself when she became aware that the very opportunities she thought she was working so hard to provide for her boys, she was actually robbing from them since if they all continued in the direction they were heading, they would not have the health to benefit from being at the best schools. She also realised that her relationship with each of them had started to suffer since she spent such little time in their company.

Has your energy been focused on your true priorities?

Now is the time to re-inject energy and attention where you most want it to go!

Purpose Statement Exercise

To help you refocus on what is most important to you in life it can be helpful to identify your underlying values and use them to create a purpose statement. A purpose statement is a combination of words that feel meaningful to you and represent the essence of what you want to focus on, nurture and prioritise in your life.

Creating a purpose statement will help you to sharpen the vision you hold for yourself for the future and pull you closer towards becoming the person you truly want to be.

Begin by highlighting any of the following values/attributes that resonate with you:

Abundance	Approachability
Acceptance	Arouse
Accessibility	Articulate
Accomplish	Artistic
Accomplishment	Assemble
Accuracy	Assertiveness
Achievement	Assist
Acknowledgement	Assurance
Acquire	Attain
Activeness	Attentive
Adaptability	Attentiveness
Adoration	Attract
Adroitness	Attractiveness
Adventure	Audacity
Affection	Augment
Affluence	Availability
Aggressiveness	Awareness
Agility	Awe
Alert	Balance
Alertness	Be accepting
Alter	Be amused
Altruism	Be awake
Ambition	Be aware
Amusement	Be bonded
Anticipation	Be connected
Appreciation	Be integrated

Be joyful
Be linked
Be passionate
Be present
Be sensitive
Be spiritual
Be the best
Be with
Beauty
Being the best
Belonging
Benevolence
Bliss
Boldness
Bravery
Brilliance
Build
Buoyancy
Calm
Calmness
Camaraderie
Candour
Capability
Capable
Care
Carefulness
Cause
Celebrity
Certainty
Challenge
Charity
Charm
Chastity
Cheerfulness

Clarity
Cleanliness
Clear-mindedness
Cleverness
Closeness
Coach
Comfort
Commitment
Community
Compassion
Compassionate
Complete
Completion
Composure
Conceive
Concentration
Confidence
Conformity
Congruency
Congruent
Connection
Consciousness
Consistency
Contentment
Continuity
Contribution
Control
Conviction
Conviviality
Coolness
Cooperation
Cordiality
Correctness
Courage

Courtesy

Craftiness

Creativity

Credibility

Cunning

Curiosity

Danger

Dare

Daring

Decisiveness

Decorum

Dedication

Deference

Delight

Dependability

Dependable

Depth

Design

Desire

Detect

Determination

Devoting

Devoutness

Dexterity

Dignity

Diligence

Direct

Direction

Directness

Discern

Discipline

Discovery

Discretion

Distinguish

Diversity

Dominance

Drama

Dream

Dreaming

Drive

Duty

Dynamism

Eagerness

Economy

Ecstasy

Educate

Education

Effectiveness

Efficiency

Elation

Elegance

Emote

Empathy

Emphasise

Encourage

Encouragement

Endeavour

Endow

Endurance

Energise

Energy

Energy flow

Enjoy

Enjoyment

Enlighten

Enrol

Entertain

Entertainment

Enthusiasm	Fortitude
Excellence	Foster
Excitement	Frankness
Exhilaration	Freedom
Expectancy	Friendliness
Expediency	Frugality
Experience	Fun
Experiment	Gallantry
Expert	Gamble
Expertise	Generosity
Explain	Gentility
Exploration	Giving
Expressiveness	Glamour
Extravagance	Govern
Extroversion	Grace
Exuberance	Grant
Facilitate	Gratitude
Fairness	Greatest
Faith	Gregariousness
Fame	Growth
Family	Guidance
Fascination	Guide
Fashion	Happiness
Fearlessness	Harmony
Ferocity	Have fun
Fidelity	Health
Fierceness	Heart
Financial independence	Helpfulness
Firmness	Heroism
Fitness	Holiness
Flexibility	Holy
Flow	Honest
Fluency	Honesty
Focus	Honour

Honouring
Hopefulness
Hospitality
Humility
Humour
Hygiene
Imagination
Impact
Impartiality
Improve
In touch with
Independence
Industry
Influence
Inform
Ingenuity
Inquisitive
Inquisitiveness
Insightfulness
Inspiration
Inspire
Instruct
Integrate
Integrity
Intelligence
Intensity
Intimacy
Intrepidness
Introversion
Intuition
Intuitiveness
Invent
Inventiveness
Investing

Joy
Judiciousness
Justice
Keenness
Kindness
Knowledge
Laugh
Leadership
Learn
Learning
Liberation
Liberty
Liveliness
Logic
Longevity
Love
Loyalty
Magnificence
Majesty
Making a difference
Mastery
Maturity
Meekness
Mellowness
Meticulousness
Mindfulness
Minister
Model
Modesty
Motivation
Move Forward
Mysteriousness
Neatness
Nerve

Obedience

Observe

Open-mindedness

Openness

Optimism

Orchestrate

Order

Organisation

Originality

Outdo

Outlandishness

Outrageousness

Passion

Patient

Peace

Peaceful

Perceive

Perceptiveness

Perfect

Perfection

Perkiness

Perseverance

Persevere

Persistence

Persuade

Persuasiveness

Philanthropy

Piety

Plan

Play games

Playful

Playfulness

Pleasantness

Pleasure

Poise

Polish

Popularity

Potency

Power

Practicality

Pragmatism

Precision

Predominate

Prepare

Preparedness

Presence

Prevail

Privacy

Proactivity

Professionalism

Prosperity

Provide

Prudence

Punctuality

Purity

Quest

Radiance

Realism

Realise

Reason

Reasonableness

Recognition

Recreation

Refine

Refinement

Reflection

Reign

Relate with God

Relaxation

Reliability

Religious

Religiousness

Resilience

Resolution

Resolve

Resourcefulness

Respect

Respond

Responsible

Rest

Restraint

Reverence

Richness

Rigour

Risk

Romance

Rule

Sacredness

Sacrifice

Sagacity

Saintliness

Sanguinity

Satisfaction

Satisfied

Score

Security

See

Seek

Self-control

Selflessness

Self-reliance

Sensation

Sense

Sensitivity

Sensual

Sensuality

Serenity

Serenity

Serve

Service

Set standards

Sex

Sexuality

Sharing

Show Compassion

Shrewdness

Significance

Silence

Silliness

Simplicity

Sincere

Sincerity

Skilfulness

Solidarity

Solitude

Soundness

Space

Spark

Speculate

Speed

Spirit

Spirituality

Spontaneity

Spontaneous

Sports

Stability

Stealth	To glow
Stillness	To lead
Stimulate	To nurture
Strength	To relate
Strengthen	To teach
Structure	To unite
Success	To win
Superiority	Touch
Support	Traditionalism
Supremacy	Tranquillity
Surprise	Transcendence
Sympathy	Transform
Synergy	Triumph
Synthesise	Trust
Taste	Trustworthiness
Teamwork	Trustworthy
Temperance	Truth
Tenderness	Turn
Thankfulness	Uncover
The Unknown	Understand
Thoroughness	Understanding
Thoughtful	Unflappability
Thoughtfulness	Unique
Thrift	Uniqueness
Thrill	Unity
Tidiness	Unstick others
Timeliness	Uplift
To catalyse	Usefulness
To contribute	Utility
To create	Valour
To discover	Variety
To experience	Venture
To feel good	Victory
To fell	Vigour

Virtue	Willingness
Vision	Win over
Vitality	Winning
Vivacity	Wisdom
Vulnerable	Wittiness
Warmth	Wonder
Watchfulness	Youthfulness
Wealth	Zeal
Wilfulness	

Next, choose the top five values/attributes that are most meaningful to you and play with them to create a statement structured in the following way:

'I am a (adjective) (nouns) who (verbs). I prioritise (xxx) so that (xxx). I value (xxx). I choose to (xxx).'

For example:

I am a generous and caring leader who inspires others to follow their passions and purpose. I prioritise my own self-care so that I can give to others from a place of plenty rather than running on empty. I value spending time with my family and friends. I choose to listen to my intuition and trust in the abundance of life.

Here are some adjectives and nouns to help you:

Example Adjectives	Astonishing
Active	Athletic
Affectionate	Attentive
Alive	Authentic
Amazing	Awesome
Amusing	Beautiful
Angelic	Big-hearted

Blissful
Bouncy
Bountiful
Brave
Bright
Brilliant
Bubbly
Buzzing
Calm
Caring
Celebrated
Cheerful
Colourful
Compassionate
Considerate
Courageous
Creative
Daring
Dazzling
Delightful
Dependable
Determined
Easy-going
Electric
Enchanted
Energetic
Excellent
Expert
Fabulous
Faithful
Fantastic
Feminine
Flowery
Fortunate

Funny
Generous
Gentle
Genuine
Gifted
Giving
Gleaming
Glistening
Glittering
Glorious
Good-natured
Gorgeous
Handsome
Happy-go-lucky
Harmonious
Healthy
Helpful
Honest
Hopeful
Humble
Humming
Ideal
Idealistic
Incredible
Intelligent
Jovial
Joyful
Juicy
Kaleidoscopic
Keen
Kindhearted
Knowledgeable
Light
Lighthearted

Likable	Safe
Lively	Sentimental
Lovable	Shimmering
Lovely	Shiny
Loving	Sociable
Lucky	Sparkling
Luminous	Striking
Lustrous	Strong
Luxurious	Stunning
Nice	Stylish
Notable	Sympathetic
Open	Talkative
Optimistic	Tender
Opulent	Terrific
Original	Thankful
Outstanding	Thoughtful
Overjoyed	Tremendous
Passionate	Trusting
Peaceful	Trustworthy
Perfect	Truthful
Playful	Unique
Pleasing	Unusual
Popular	Upbeat
Positive	Valuable
Powerful	Vast
Precious	Velvety
Quick-witted	Vibrant
Quirky	Virtuous
Quizzical	Vital
Radiant	Vivacious
Ready	Warmhearted
Reliable	Wealthy
Respectful	Well-groomed
Rich	Wide-eyed

Willing
Witty
Wonderful
Worthwhile
Young
Youthful
Yummy
Zesty

Example Nouns

Academic
Acrobat
Actor
Angel
Architect
Artist
Athlete
Believer
Billionaire
Bookworm
Brother
Businessman/
Businesswoman
Butterfly
Carer
Champion
Cheerleader
Coach
Companion
Creator
Dancer
Daughter
Designer

Director
Doctor
Dolphin
Dreamer
Eagle
Economist
Editor
Engineer
Entertainer
Expert
Fairy
Father
Friend
Gardener
Gift
Giver
Grandparent
Grasshopper
Guider
Gymnast
Gypsy
Hedonist
Helper
Hero
Hippy
Hummingbird
Husband
Illuminator
Intellectual
Jewel
Juggler
Kestrel
Kingfisher
Knight

Lady

Leader

Linguist

Lion

Listener

Lover

Luminary

Magician

Maiden

Maker of Dreams

Man

Manager

Master

Matron

Mediator

Messenger

Midwife

Millionaire

Mother

Motivator

Musician

Negotiator

Orchid

Owl

Parent

Peace Maker

Peacock

Pearl

Performer

Philosopher

Physician

Pilot

Player

Playwright

Poet

Politician

Prince

Princess

Problem Solver

Professor

Programmer

Public Speaker

Pupil

Racehorse

Rainbow

Role Model

Sailor

Seahorse

Shell

Sister

Son

Star

Student

Surfer

Surprise

Surveyor

Swan

Teacher

Team Leader

Team Player

Tiger

Trainer

Tree

Winner

Woman

Writer

Creating Your Future Vision

Pain pushes us until vision pulls us.
Michael Beckworth

Connecting with a clear future vision can truly help to keep you aligned with the brilliance you have within and prevent you from reverting to any of your old burnout habits or patterns.

One of the best techniques I've discovered for helping people articulate their deepest desires for the future involves following a guided meditation process based on techniques created by Future Life Progression pioneer and metaphysical teacher, Anne Jirsch.[65] I deeply respect and recommend her work. A complimentary audio recording of a teleseminar I hosted with Anne is available at www.jaynemorris.com.

Future Life Progression (FLP) is a tool that can help you take a snapshot of your future to gain valuable life learning. It works in a similar way to the techniques used in the corporate world when executives gather and brainstorm products or services they might offer in the future and creative ways to remain competitive in the marketplace.

FLP is a simple psychological process that can help us envision future possibilities and life scenarios. It can help give you more clarity and certainty about what directions to take and decisions to make.

When you perceive possible future scenarios, you can see, hear, and feel that futuristic information... you then store this information about the future event... with the information later becoming available as memory.
Dr Atwater

FLP has helped my clients gain crystal clear understanding and insight that has proven invaluable when designing the life they really want to live in the future. Many credit the process for opening up their awareness to new ideas, new ways of thinking, career paths they previously hadn't considered and business approaches unheard of in their industry.

What follows is a simplified version of a guided *Future Vision Expansion Meditation* to help you to uncover as much of your future vision as possible.

Vision Expansion Exercise

This exercise will help you explore, with gratitude, what it is that you would love to be, do and have in the future.

Grab a pen and paper and write down whatever you think or feel in response to the following questions:

What would you want to be, do, have or create if:

- You knew it was ok to have anything you wanted?
- You knew you deserved it?
- You had full support of others?
- You knew you could succeed?
- You had abundant resources?
- You had all the confidence in the world?
- You had all the money you needed and all the time you needed?

If you woke tomorrow morning to find all these things had arrived in your life, what else would you *really* desire? (State what you want in positive terms – e.g., 'I would have a fit and healthy body', *not* 'I would no longer be fat and unhealthy'.)

Write or draw your response.

Now ask yourself 'what *more* do I want?'. Keep asking yourself if there is anything else, until all of your deepest, most heartfelt passions and desired have been allowed to surface.

Write or draw your response.

Finally, respond to the following questions:

- What do you most deeply desire to experience in your life?
- What do you most deeply desire to express?
- What do you most deeply desire to create in your life?
- What do you most deeply desire to contribute?
- What is at stake if you ignore these desires?
- What is possible for you if you trust and follow these desires?
- What is your deepest intention for the year ahead?
- How will you know when you have what you want?
- What will you feel, see, hear and believe about yourself?

Future Vision Expansion Meditation

Before beginning this meditation take some time to relax and unwind. Sit somewhere that you feel safe, comfortable and will not be disturbed. Turn off your cell phone. Have a shawl or blanket nearby in case you get cold.

Depending on your preferred learning style you may choose simply to read and follow the meditation as it is written below or to listen to it as a recording (www.jaynemorris.com).

You may wish to close your eyes and focus on the images, words, phrases, inner knowing or feelings as if experiencing them as a journey within yourself or alternatively you may wish to keep your eyes open and have coloured pastels or a pen and some paper to hand so that you can draw or write as understanding, inspiration and guidance flows to you.

The meditation will help you to explore the sensation of being, doing and having all the things you would most love to experience in your life. You will be guided to anchor those feelings so that when you return to the present moment, after the meditation, you will feel confident in being able to reconnect with the energy of the experience any time you choose.

Whenever you return to the feelings experienced during this meditation you realign your energy with the positive intention of manifesting your deepest desires in the future. The act of doing this raises your energetic vibration and helps you to attract to you all the corresponding opportunities, people, places and experiences that match your desires for your highest good and for the highest good and betterment of the lives of others.

FLP can be particularly helpful when exploring a new business or career direction because it helps to open your imagination to options that you might not otherwise have explored or entertained.

The technique helps you to explore possible paths for the future. In doing so, the insight and inner guidance that you receive then becomes part of your conscious awareness. Your brain registers the fact that any information pertaining to your visualisations is relevant and communicates this with your reticular activating system (RAS). Your RAS is a part of your brain that acts as a filter between your conscious and subconscious.

Have you ever noticed, just after buying a new car, that you seem to see other people driving the same make or model on every street? That is an example of your RAS in action. Another would be when you first discover that you or your partner is pregnant and suddenly you see pregnant women wherever you go.

The process of FLP brings new information into your conscious awareness and your RAS helps you to seek out evidence and opportunities to support your goals and to realise the positive outcomes experienced in your visualisations. This in effect helps to bring things in ahead of time.

It is not just the RAS of the brain that remembers the details experienced during FLP. Science indicates that the very cellular structures of our body hold this information in the same way that it holds memories of past events.

Dr Atwater writes about future awareness in her book, *Future Memory*. She references Professor Peter Derks, a specialist in memory research at the College of William and Mary in Virginia,

USA, who suggests that all memories are stored 'not just in the brain' or mind, but in the cellular structures of our body. In summary:

> *Whatever is perceived during any state of consciousness is remembered. By recalling that memory, a former state of consciousness can be re-experienced – past, present, or future.*
> Dr Atwater

When using a tool like FLP to visualise a future event we essentially create new, positive intentions, which are stored, like memories by our body and brain. This means that our FLP memories can then be purposefully accessed, recalled and re-experienced to help us stay positively motivated and take inspired action towards our goals for the future.

I have created the *Future Vision Expansion Meditation* is such a way that you can completely relax and enjoy the experience, safe in the knowledge that your subconscious mind and higher self will only show or give you a sense of experiences that are for your highest learning and understanding, that are aligned with your highest good and that you are ready to have brought into your conscious awareness.

Remember, whatever you think in your mind and believe about yourself affects your physical body, your emotions, behaviour and ultimately your overall experience of life.

> *Begin by bringing your focus to your breath. Take a full, deep breath all way down into your abdomen. Allow yourself to breathe, just like a baby, by gently expanding and contracting your abdomen. Rest your awareness on each breath and allow your body to relax more and more deeply.*
>
> *Notice how soft and relaxed your breathing has become. Focus on breathing in a sense of calm and breathing out any feelings of tension.*

Take your attention to the top of your head and imagine a gentle waterfall of pure white light flowing down to the top of your head, relaxing all the little muscles of your scalp.

Feel the light flowing into your head, bathing you in warmth and relaxation. Sense that light calming and relaxing your forehead, smoothing away any lines caused by stress or tension. Allow the light to soothe your eyelids, your eyes and all the surrounding muscles.

Sense the light relaxing the back of your head. Feel it gently easing and relaxing all of the muscles in your face and head, softening your mind and softening your body.

Feel the beautiful light flowing down now into your cheeks, moving slowly and gently into your mouth, your jaw, your teeth, your tongue. Feel the warmth softening your lips and gently relaxing your chin. Allow the feeling of relaxation to spread into your neck, soothing all the muscles at the front and the sides and the back of your neck.

Sense waves of contentment rippling out across your shoulders, relaxing all the muscles at the top of your arms. Feel it rolling down your upper arms and elbows, right down through your lower arms, your wrists and hands and right to the tips of your fingers.

Feel the white light spreading out across your back, easing every ligament. Releasing any tension. Send the warmth of the light all the way down your back. Relax more and more deeply.

Feel a growing sense of comfort spreading down through your chest and the entire trunk of your body. Relax into your hips, into your stomach and your buttocks. Vizualise this sensation of relaxation flowing down your legs, into your knees, your calves, your ankles and right the way down to the tips of your toes.

Notice how the beautiful white light is continuously moving and bathing you in a relaxation. Feel the light continuously flowing through you and washing over you, all the way from the top of your head down across your face, down your throat and chest, down into your lower abdomen, into the top of your legs and right down to your toes. Then flowing back up your legs, all the way along your spine, up to your neck and head, over the top of your head and back down your face again, back down through your arms and body, down through your hips, your legs, across your knees, down your shins.

With each exhalation release any tensions to this white light and sensing and stress, worry or fears being transmuted by this light.

Sense that you are safe and protected by this light.

As you breathe in, breathe in the sense of peace and protection that the light gives you.

Set an intention now to connect with a vision of your future, five years on from now, having changed the trajectory of your life from one previously burdened by old patterns of burnout to one powerfully aligned with your inner brilliance.

Imagine now that you are lying on a very comfortable, beautiful bed and that the beautiful white light is surrounding you and the bed.

Notice as the light shimmers and sparkles around the bed, lifting it up very gently, lifting you up and out of the room, up above the town or city where you live, up higher into the sky, up into the clouds, sensing beautiful clouds all around you and becoming aware of the bed transporting you forward now into your future.

Sense your bed moving gently forward in time, moving one year ahead into the future, two years, three years, four years, then slowing down as you reach five years ahead in your life.

Feel the bed softly moving down through the clouds, back down towards the earth, gently moving down, placing you in a new scene. A scene from your future five years, the future ahead of you that you have created as a result of following your intuition, prioritising self-care, honouring your true desires, pursuing your passions and trusting fully in yourself and your abilities.

Use all of your senses to gently adjust yourself to this new scene.

Start to become aware of how you are feeling in your body, what you sense about this scene, what you know about it, what you can hear, see, smell.

Where are you? What does this place you find yourself in feel like?

Are you indoors or outside?

Allow the information to flow to you in whatever form it takes.

You may sense feelings in your body, see images in your mind's eye, hear a whispering of an inner voice or gain an understanding about this place that simply drops into your conscious awareness.

Explore the surroundings you find yourself in and gain further understanding about whether this is somewhere you live, work or spend time doing other things.

Stay with the sensations you get in your body, the images you see, the sounds or words you hear and any sense of inner knowing or understanding as it drops into your awareness.

What does it feel your day-to-day life is like?

Who do you share most of your time with?

Focus in on the information as it comes to you.

What is your health like now that you take better care of yourself?

How is your work?

What kind of projects or areas do you work in or on?

Allow the answers to come.

Give yourself permission to connect you now with the insight and understanding that your future self would like to share with you about what is possible for you in your life when you truly align with your inner brilliance.

What does he or she most want you to know? Wait for the response.

It may come as a symbol, as a word or phrase, as a feeling, or again, as an inner knowing.

Focus on anything else you would like to know from this time.

Take a moment to ask any questions that you would like to have answered. Just allow the answers and guidance to flow to you.

Thank your future self for sharing his/her wisdom with you. Feel the positive energy of the future you. Notice what colour that energy has and soak it right up inside of you. Breathe it in and really fill yourself with it. Feel it replenish and re-energise every cell of your body. Take your non-dominant hand and place it over the part of your body where you feel that energy vibrating the strongest.

Know that at any time you need to top up on that energy, you can do so just by placing your hand on that part of your body and setting the intention to connect with that energy again.

You can tap into this energy at any time, whenever you wish. It is already part of you. It is already within you.

This energy is infinite so you can soak up as much as you wish.

Keep this energy with you and gently bring your awareness back to your breath.

Take three full, deep breaths and purposefully bring your attention back to your physical body, being present in the here and now, easing yourself back to a full awareness of being back in the room, your feet flat on the floor.

Gently move your fingers and toes, stretch your arms and legs and slowly open your eyes feeling refreshed, revitalised and ready to take positive action towards creating the future that you were born to live.

Meaningful Mornings

The key to harnessing the power of your *Future Vision Expansion Meditation* experience is to regularly replay the feelings you gained when surrounded by the positive energy of your future life aligned with your inner brilliance. This enables you to live the life of your dreams starting right now.

I encourage my clients to create a daily morning ritual to purposefully help them focus their attention on raising and maintaining their energetic vibration, reconnect with the essence of their future vision and set an inspiring intention for the day ahead.

Meaningful rituals are the key difference between a world that can sometimes be confusing and a world that merges your mind, body, and spirit as one.
Janet Attwood

Rituals can be found at the very foundations of every ancient culture, yet their significance today is often overlooked. Many old rituals have been lost in postmodern life, but the essence of an incredible number remain and are evident in grieving ceremonies, celebrations of the milestones of life, the Olympic traditions passed down from the Greeks and so on.

Human beings naturally gravitate toward rituals: the way we comb or brush our hair, the route we take to work, the things we do when we take a chance on something, or how we prepare for a big competition, presentation, or meeting.

When we switch off our autopilot and perform a routine with intention and purpose we transform our habits into sources of inspiration and bring about measurable impactful results. The results of a recent sports psychology study indicated clear performance benefits of pre-performance rituals, including improved attention and increased emotional stability and confidence.[66]

After 15 years as a popular singer and songwriter, Christine Kane says that she harnessed the power of purposeful morning rituals to help her change career direction and create Uplevel You, a million-dollar company committed to the growth and empowerment of entrepreneurs and creative individuals around the globe.

She recalls how she used to be a 'creature of zero habits' without much direction or focus. Creating rituals helped her consciously choose to *create* her day, rather than *reacting* to it. She says that her morning ritual sets the tone for not just her day, or her productivity, but for her life. She combines a mixture of physical, mental and heart-centered activities to engage these human power centers.

Christine drinks pure water upon waking in order to help positively support the physiological functions of her body through proper hydration. Before getting out of bed she takes a moment to silently create a mental gratitude list. Next she spends some time moving her body. After exercising she meditates and sets an intention for the day. Finally, she eats something healthy and nutritious to set the stage for a successful day ahead.

It is natural to resist the concept of introducing a ritual into your daily life when you desperately seek to reduce your to-do list rather than add to it. Relax. I have found a creative way around this, which my clients claim works extremely well. Simply transform the time you usually spend each morning doing something routine like taking a shower or brushing your teeth into a conscious morning ritual.

You can begin this tomorrow. Instead of leaping out of bed when the alarm clock startles you, checking your phone for news, messages, and emails, running over the day's to-do list in your mind and filling your head with fears about how you are going to fit everything in and get through the day when your body feels like a lead balloon, imagine doing things a little differently.

Visualise yourself taking a moment tomorrow morning *before* getting out of bed to check in with how you are feeling and gently appreciate your body. Imagine focusing your attention on the part of you that most feels alive and inviting the feeling you have in that area to expand and spread out across the rest of your body.

Picture yourself turning your awareness to your breath and taking three full, deep breathes to re-oxygenate your body; then ease it slowly out of bed. Imagine stretching your arms and legs and consciously bringing yourself into the body that will be supporting you today.

Purposefully use the time when you take your shower, make your morning cup of tea or brush your teeth to bring to mind the memories you created during your experience of the *Future Vision Expansion Meditation*. Recall the feelings you had in your body when you experienced yourself five years on in the future with your deepest desires having already manifested. Harness that energy and allow it to help you set a positive intention for the day. Ask your inner guidance: 'What one quality can I bring to my day today for my highest good?' Allow an answer to flow to you and give you inspiration to carry you through the day ahead.

You can boost your morning ritual by adding music, looking at an inspiring image or vision board, incorporating the power shout, singing or some form of conscious body movement. Have fun with it and prepare to feel it powerfully affect your everyday experience.

Creating a Vision Board

Vision boards are fast being recognised as more than just a bit of creative fun and credited by leaders of our time a powerful tool for transformation.

Notable celebrities including Olympian Rueben Gonzalez, Jim Carey, Oprah Winfrey, and Arnold Schwarzenegger frequently reference the important role that creative visioning has played in the realisation of their dreams.

When I was very young I visualized myself being and having what it was I wanted. Mentally I never had any doubts about it. The mind is really so incredible. Before I won my first Mr. Universe title, I walked around the tournament like I owned it. The title was already mine. I had won it so many times in my mind that there was no doubt I would win it. Then when I moved on to the movies, the same thing. I visualized myself being a famous actor and earning big money. I could feel and taste success. I just knew it would all happen.
Arnold Schwarzenegger

Vision Boards are a modern manifestation method combining concepts taken from creative hobbies like scrapbooking with motivational mind-mapping and brand development techniques used by marketeers.

A vision board is quite literally a collage of pictures, phrases, poems and quotes that visually represent what you would like to experience more of in your life. The reason they can be extremely effective is that, when used regularly, they help to strengthen higher order in psychological constructs of psychological capital. Psychological capital is defined as the 'positive and developmental state of an individual as characterized by high self-efficacy, optimism, hope and resiliency'.[67]

Studies conducted by leading professors at the W.P. Carey School of Business School in Arizona show that when psychological capital is nurtured, individual employee performance is increased. They also suggest that strengthening these characteristics in top executives has a team-level impact on organisational performance.[68]

As I mentioned in the art experiment section of this book, creative exercises can help us to increase self-awareness and externalise our internal existence. The physical process of creating a vision board can be extremely powerful in uncovering hidden desires and making contact with inner guidance to help clarify the details for the road map of your future.

Some people are initially hesitant to take time out to experiment in making a vision board, especially if they don't naturally think of themselves as a 'creative type'. If this is happening for you, then I want to reassure you that *anyone* can create a powerful board. Devoting a few hours to the process will be time well spent because the results that follow are often truly profound.

When created in alignment with one's true values, positive beliefs, inspired goals, positive intentions, heartfelt aspirations and an attitude of gratitude, vision boards support not just positive thinking but crucially also support the development of inspired strategies and goal setting, providing a plan for the positive action-taking required to bring about desired results.

The order of the exercises in this book have been purposefully presented to best help you clear and prepare your energy and mindset so that you are ready to create a board that corresponds with the highest vision your heart holds for you, rather than an ego-directed shopping list.

I have been running vision board workshops and courses for several years, and participants never cease to surprise me with their ingenuity when creating their boards and the powerful transformations they experience as a result of using their boards to help them stay focused and inspired in their lives.

You may wish to put pictures that you have drawn or painted on your board. Alternatively, they may all come from external sources like magazines and brochures or images that you have found online. Regardless of the source, the key to creating a truly powerful board is to use your inner navigation system to help you intuitively select images and phrases that most inspire you.

I recommend allowing about three hours in total for the creation of your board, so that you can do it at a relaxed pace, without feeling rushed. Some people finish much quicker than this; some feel they need a little longer.

Here is a breakdown of a guideline for timings:

- 30 Minutes – Preparing Space
- 1 Hour – Tearing Out Images
- 1 Hour – Sorting Through and Positioning Images
- 30 Minutes – Sticking Down/Fixing in Place

The most popular formats for vision boards are:

- **Intuitive Board** – Stick what you want, wherever you best feel it goes.
- **Mandala** – meaning 'circle' in Sanskrit. Position your

images, words, and phrases in a circular format.

- **Balance Wheel Board** – Section your board into separate areas using the different segment titles of the *Balance Wheel* exercise featured earlier in this book as a guide.

One of my previous workshop participants, Juliette Jeanclaude, Founder of Healing Creativity, is a big fan of mandalas and uses them a lot in her work as an artist and creative coach. She says creating something in a circle helps her to focus, relax, and centre herself. By centring herself she says she is more able to love who she is. She wanted to fill her board with that vibration of love, hence, why she chose to create her board as a mandala:

The images I picked up were just perfect, because before searching for them I cleared out lots of mental clutter and was able to focus my intention and on what I really need. My Vision Board makes me feel so so good – It makes me feel at peace and helps me laugh everyday.

To create her mandala Juliette positioned all her images and phrases in a circle. At the centre she put a small circle of pink card with a heart inside it and a beautiful white flower. She then added her photograph above the flower when she returned home after the workshop.

7 Simple Steps to Create Your Board

1. **Board Basics** – Choose a large piece of card, poster board, corkboard or canvas about the size of a large newspaper opened out. Your board needs to be big enough to spaciously arrange your selected words and images.

Gather approximately 10-20 assorted magazines. Use a variety of genres, (e.g., House & Home, Woman's Glossies, Spiritual, Men's Magazines, Health & Fitness, and Hobbies). Include a few travel magazines into the mix which are great for images of animals that can often represent qualities you would like to embrace more of and that uplift and inspire, energise or relax you. Hair and beauty salons, libraries and community centres are often happy to clear out old magazines.

You will also need pens, scissors, glue or pins, sticky tape and a current photograph of yourself.

Many people find that there is something incredibly cathartic about creating a board using their hands. However, some people prefer to create their board using a computer. Both methods work well.

2. **Prepare a Space** – Find somewhere quiet where you can be undisturbed and completely relaxed. Prepare a special space to work on your board. Gather all the materials you need together so that they are within easy reach. Do whatever it takes to make the space feel as comfortable and special as possible. Play some uplifting music without lyrics. Place a vase of fresh flowers in the area. Light a candle. Wear clothes that you feel good in. Open a window and allow fresh air to circulate through your space to shift any stagnant energy.

3. **Mindset Magic** – Let go of anything you feel you 'should, ought to, or must' aspire towards. Give yourself permission to explore the things that *you* really want to welcome more of in

your life. Review your responses to the exercises that you have completed as part of this section of the book to help guide you towards images, words and phrases that are aligned with the things you really value and want to focus on, prioritise and develop in your life.

If you receive the inspiration and feel the desire to be, do, or have something in your life, then you absolutely can make it happen – even if you do not yet know how. As Walt Disney once said, 'If you can dream it, you can do it.' Believe in the possibility of your dreams becoming reality for you. Believe that you are entitled to them. Fill your board with the energy of those dreams and the excitement and anticipation that they bring you.

4. **Flick, Snip and Stick** – Have fun flicking through magazines (or searching online) for images and words that inspire you. Tear or cut out anything that jumps out at you and make a pile of clippings. When you feel you have enough images, begin your board, put the magazines to one side and sit for a few minutes sorting through your images.

You do not need to know what the image represents for you at this stage. Simply focus on keeping all the images you love looking at and trust your intuition on any pictures that do not feel *right*. Sift through the pile so that only the images and words that really inspire you remain.

5. **Arrange** – experiment by positioning the images, words and phrases on your board in whatever way feels good. Once you are happy with the positioning of your various images it is useful to take a snapshot of your board using a digital camera. Images can easily move when you start sticking, so having this photo will help you remember where they each go as you start to glue or tape them down.

There is no right or wrong way to secure your images. Some people like them to be easily changeable – fixed with scotch tape or drawing pins. Others like them to be pasted down with glue and varnished for a professional-looking finish. Trust your gut feeling.

The important thing is to arrange your images with plenty of space in between, symbolising your intention to stay open to receiving more!

When you have finished your board place your purpose statement accompanied by a current photo of yourself at the centre of your board to symbolise you being the creator of your experience.

In addition to having a photo of yourself in the middle of the board, you can also add photos of yourself to some of your chosen images, (e.g., at the steering wheel of your racing car picture or in the middle of the image of a safari scene). This can add extra power to your board because it visually helps you put yourself in the board.

6. **Position with Pride** – Proudly display your board somewhere in your home or office where you are most active during the day and will see it regularly (even if this is from your peripheral vision). Ideally position it at eye level in a space that is in alignment with your vision – i.e., not above your toilet or inside a cupboard! An alternative to hanging it on a wall is to take a photograph of it and use it as a screensaver on your computer, laptop or Smartphone.

The more time you spend with your board the more movement you will make toward your goals, and the faster they will manifest into reality.

Ensure the space around your board supports your vision; clear away any clutter or things that don't reflect the words and images on your board.

7. **Activate Your Board** – Once you have completed your board, take some time to sit with it and connect with the images, words

and phrases positioned on it. Visualise yourself being, doing, having and experiencing all the things on your board as if they are already part of your life. State your purpose statement to yourself – out loud if possible.

Anytime when you feel like you need a break you can use your board to help you take a mini mind-holiday. Simply settle yourself somewhere comfy and allow yourself to take an imaginary journey into one of the images on the board. For example:

- Explore what it feels like to be the dolphin in the picture you cut out or how it feels to stand at the top of the mountain in your health section.
- Visualise yourself having dinner with the man of your dreams.
- Experiment with what it feels like to live in that house you would love.
- Play with the sensation of sparkling and shining like the diamond in your wealth section.

Allow your vision board to be a continuously moving creation with room to add more images as your ideas develop and change. Whenever you bring something on your board into being celebrate and express gratitude for this success.

You may like to keep a gratitude journal to acknowledge positive things as they come into your life, or alternatively pop a little smiley face or tick mark next to the corresponding image, word or phrase whenever you notice it has manifested itself.

In my experience, it also helps to share your board with those who are supportive of you. Sharing your board helps you declare your desires externally, the process of which makes them feel more real and therefore more attainable.

If you have the opportunity to attend one of my future vision board workshops or retreats, then I encourage you to use that as an opportunity to experience how wonderful it is to have your board received by others in an open, caring and nurturing space. I also facilitate activities where participants read their purpose statements to each other, which is extremely powerful.

People who experience most success with their vision boards practice visualising already having all the things they want to be, do, have and create in their lives regularly – *every day*. Include looking at your board as part of your morning ritual.

What I love, and what is so powerful about these inspirational, uplifting boards, is that because they come from inside you and are guided by your own inner longings, they are powerful tools for inspiration and change...I use mine as ways of shifting mood, appreciating myself more, and creating gratitude for where I am – as well as for supporting my vision of myself in the future. Other people see them and become inspired too.

Elese Coit

Setting Inspired Goals

Many people set goals that they fail to achieve because they have made them based on things they think they should do, rather than from heartfelt desires. New Year's resolutions are a good example of this because they tend to be fuelled with negative energy. Approaching the start of a new year in this way feels depressing and draining. No wonder people find themselves year after year setting identical resolutions to the ones they failed to keep several years in succession.

Inspired goals work differently. They involve setting yourself targets that feel truly energising and inspiring. This process can be extremely powerful in helping you stay focused and move forward towards your dreams.

New Beliefs

It can be extremely beneficial to use your vision board to help you set inspired goals and develop a future strategy for sustaining your energy and actions towards your vision. To do this, begin by using your board to help you reaffirm any new beliefs that you want to hold in order to do things differently in your life to bring about new, improved results.

Here is a coaching exercise to help get you started:

Q: What would you need to believe to act *right now*, as if you already have/experience/live all of the things that your board represents?

A: 'To believe I can lead the life I want and have all of the things on my board, I need to affirm to myself that I . . .'

(State your answers using positive language and in the present tense – i.e., 'I am confident', 'I have all the resources within me', 'I can make friends easily'.)

New Actions

Albert Einstein famously defined insanity as 'doing the same thing over and over again and expecting different results'. If you took action aligned with your new beliefs, what ten things might you do differently on a daily basis? What risks might you take? What might you say to whom? What would you say no to when you usually say yes? How would you be a shade braver?

Goal-Setting Exercise

There is no one giant step that does it. It's a lot of little steps.
Peter A. Cohen

Sometimes, when people dream big they subsequently stop themselves from taking action because they feel like the distance between them and their goal is too big. Any goal is achievable when we break it down into a series of small, manageable steps.

The next exercise will help you to use your board to set goals. After you have set them, I encourage you to map out what do-able actions you could take to get started in the direction of your dreams. Commit to taking the first small step as soon as possible; this will help to beat procrastination and act as a catalyst for further action towards your desires.

Use your board to help you answer the following questions. They are designed to help you explore each of the words, images and phrases on your board and set inspired goals from them.

- Which image or phrase stands out to you the most?
- What do you notice about this image or phrase that surprises or intrigues you?
- What do you think or feel when you look at this phrase or picture?
- What indication does this give you about what you would like to experience more of in your life?

- What goal could you set in relation to this?
- What strengths and skills do you already have that could help you reach this goal?
- What connections or contacts might be able to support you?
- Are there any barriers between you and this goal?
- How might you be able to overcome them?
- What new information, tools, techniques or trainings might you need to help you achieve this goal?
- What ten simple things could you do to help you get started in the direction of your goal?
- What is the first step you could take towards your goal?
- When are you going to take it?
- What else are you going to do and when, in order to reach this goal?
- What actions are you going to take – beginning tomorrow – towards your dreams?

Action is the great equalizer. No matter how difficult things may seem and no matter how large the task, there's always something which can be done.
Michael Neill

Future Action Map

If the process of creating a board has proven to be enjoyable for you, then you may wish to consider mapping out a plan of action in a visual way to help keep the process feel inspiring. There are no hard and fast rules for this; simply follow your creative flow and give yourself permission for your action map to take form, in any shape or design that appeals to your imagination.

You may wish to sketch out your future action map in an art book, doodle it on design paper or construct another board style masterpiece of your plan. If you have a goal that takes the form of a business plan or big project then you might enjoy reading

Jennifer Lee's book, *The Right Brained Business Plan*, to help spark off further ideas and inspiration. You can download a podcast of an interview I hosted with her on this very topic at the website for this book: www.jaynemorris.com.

Alternatively, if you enjoy taking a more analytical and logical approach to things, then you may prefer to plan things out by taking a more traditional approach. Again, there is no right or wrong; map away in your own preferred style until your heart is content.

Balance Action with Inaction

Many people suffering burnout do not have a problem getting things done or taking action. In fact, it is their proactive addiction that often led to them to doing too much and burning out in the first place. If this rings true with your former tendencies, beware of repeating old patterns.

Being constantly busy and overscheduled is not necessarily a sign of efficiency. As Juan Somavia, ILO Director-General, states: 'While the benefits of hard work are clear, working more is not the same as working better.'

Busyness can be procrastination in disguise. When you notice you are filling your time being constantly busy, but not making progress on the tasks you really need to get done, identify what you are avoiding, take a break, list any non-urgent and non-necessary distractions that you can cut out and explore creative solutions to help you move forward.

As I noted earlier *Extreme Self-care*, it is important to carve out thinking time and protect your rest and relaxation. Not only will this help you balance action with inaction, but it will also help you generate genius ideas and supercharge your productivity.

Wellness Balance Chart

Balance often comes from the wisdom to take something away when we add something on.
Anne Wilson Schaef

I often encourage my clients to think of their energy like their bank account. Just as you aim to balance income and expenditure with your bank account, for every action step taken that requires you to expend energy there needs to be a non-action or wellness action to avoid energy debt and ensure you maintain energy credit.

The overall aim is to always have some reserve credit for unforeseen demands so that you have sufficient energy in your account to handle anything non-goal related that happens during your day and causes you to withdraw more from your account than planned.

If at any time you notice your energy withdrawals are greater than your deposits and, as a result, you have a negative account balance, schedule in extra self-care to bring your account back into credit.

The Wellness Balance Chart in Table 3.2 (found at the end of this chapter) can help you to keep track and acknowledge your successes. Record the date, followed by a description of your energy transaction, then a figure representing how much energy your transaction has deposited or withdrawn, and finally your total balance.

Set figures for deposits and withdrawals that *feel* right for you. I suggest using rounded numbers in the 100s to keep it simple.

An example of how it works is in Table 3.1.

Use Table 3.2 to help you keep track and acknowledge your successes. You can find a downloadable version of this chart on the website: www.jaynemorris.com.

Be Patient

A note of caution: your old burnout programming of rushing to get everything done at once and expecting miraculous results overnight is likely to try to rear its ugly head from time to time. When you notice yourself buying into an illusion of urgency, remind yourself that it is okay to slow down and take a slower, steadier approach. This is a new life style you are committing to leading, not a race that you are running.

Progress is not measured in miles, it is measured in inches. Do not wonder why things are "taking so long." In fact, everything is rolling out exactly as it needs to, using not a minute more than Perfection requires. Rest easy and be at peace. Life is working its magic even as you take your very next breath. There. See? You could almost feel the Perfection, couldn't you?
Neale Donald Walsch

Fuel for Brilliance

Your new brilliant life is ready and waiting for you!

Before you boldly leap forward I encourage you to reflect on all that we've covered together and consider what key practices, people, places and things are going to sustain you.

What help might you need, what more skills might you want to develop and what other things might you need to consider?

Strategies for Sustained Success

The exercises you've completed in this book have helped you identify, release and change the old beliefs that kept you stuck in an experience of burnout. You now are ready to create a new vision for your future. Transformation can happen quickly, but in order to prevent old patterns of burnout creeping back in again, it is important to fully commit to making your health and well-being a priority.

The following strategies for sustained success will help you stay aligned with your true inner brilliance. They have been utilised by CEOs, organisational leaders and celebrities with whom I've consulted over the years – and they work!

Get Enough Sleep

As previously highlighted, sleep is vital for your body to rest, repair and reset itself. It brings benefits to physical and emotional well-being and cognitive functioning. Although the National Sleep Foundation suggest that most adults need an average of 7-9 hours of sleep daily, many barely manage half that amount. According to American physician Dr Charles Czeisler, sleeping four or five hours per night induces mental impairment equivalent to a blood alcohol level above the legal driving limit.[69]

Strategic Renewal – including… longer sleep hours, more time away from the office and longer, more frequent vacations – boosts productivity, job performance, and, of course, health.
Tony Schwartz

Help yourself get better rest by:

- adjusting your bedtime gradually so that it is 20 minutes earlier each week, until you are going to bed at a time that ensures you get enough sleep before your alarm wakens

you in the morning
- leaving your smart phone outside the bedroom
- relaxing for 30 minutes before bed
- keeping your bedroom clear of clutter
- avoiding caffeine before bed
- reducing the temperature of your bedroom

Power Naps

I used to sleep in taxis. You've got to make a judgment: is this environment best for sleeping, working, or do I need to forego this time. It's always about balance.... I can't tell you how many times I've slept at a desk, on the floor, in a cab, just a few minutes to be able to keep going.
Paul Engel, Knowledge Capital Consulting

Experiment with power naps. Various studies show that naps can restore wakefulness,[70] promote performance and learning,[71] help regulate hormones, elevate your mood, aid weight loss, enhance your sex life, improve stamina and strengthen memory.[72]

Research indicates that a short 10-20 minute snooze is optimum.[73] However, it is best to trial naps of varied lengths to find your own preferred duration. I am a strong advocate of making naps acceptable in the workplace as a means for people to top up their energy during their breaks.

How realistic is it for people to sleep at work? It all seems to depend on what country you live and work in. The Spanish have long been known to take restorative siestas in the middle of the day. In Japan, staff often take a snooze to help sustain themselves when working long hours, and in the US forward-thinking companies like the Huffington Post, AOL, Google, and Cisco provide places specifically for their employees to go and rejuvenate by catching 40 winks.

If I take a nap and I have a tiny slice of frozen chocolate chip cookie dough, I'm a better woman.
Ali Wentworth

In the UK however, the concept of power naps has until now been met with some resistance. Throughout history, however, some of the greatest leaders both in Britain and across the pond have attributed their sustained success to the routine of taking a nap. In Churchill's words:

Nature has not intended mankind to work from eight in the morning until midnight without that refreshment of blessed oblivion which, even if it only lasts 20 minutes, is sufficient to renew all vital forces.

A cultural shift to make napping acceptable in the workplace could help corporations gain the competitive advantage during tough economic times. In order for the benefits of power naps to be realised, change must come (as it often does) from the top down, so if you want to be more productive this afternoon, offer a copy of this book to your boss to help convince her of the benefits that napping can bring.

How to take a power nap:

- **Be Creative** – Naps can be taken almost anytime, any place, if you get creative. An associate of Thomas Edison claimed that his genius for sleep equaled his genius for invention. He could sleep anywhere, anytime, on anything. Keep a pillow under your desk and look for an empty meeting room at lunchtime. If everything appears occupied try finding a space at the back of a nearby yoga or Pilates class so you can nod off for a while undisturbed.
- **Feel Safe** – Our primal instincts can prevent us taking a nap if we are sensitive sleepers and don't feel relaxed in our environment. Do what you can to reduce distractions;

if you have your own office, lock the door, pop in some earplugs, wear an eye mask or close the blinds.

- **Set an Alarm** – You will relax and drift off more easily if you know that you are not going to sleep through an important meeting or miss the last stop on the bus. Set an alarm to wake you up after 20-30 minutes.
- **Avoid Caffeine** – Caffeine disturbs sleep. For your nap to have the best effect, avoid drinking caffeine four to five hours before you snooze.
- **Permission** – Release any inner gremlins telling you that you are 'lazy' for napping. Remind yourself of the benefits.

Yoga Nidra

During the summer of 2013 I was invited to be a guest speaker and mentor on Karen Brody's Feminine Leap Programme – a 40-day course for people wanting to rebalance their mental, physical, spiritual, and emotional health. As part of the programme participants were taught an ancient Indian relaxation process called *Yoga Nidra*.

Yoga Nidra is a form of power napping. It is a deep conscious sleep-like state that can be achieved by following a guided meditation led by an experienced practitioner. It is like taking an inward journey, which helps to connect you with your deepest desires and a greater awareness of your inner resources, physical sensations, breath, energy, feelings, emotions and sense of self.

You don't 'do' yoga nidra – it just happens. It does YOU.
Kamini Desai

To practice Yoga Nidra you need a comfortable place to lie down, a blanket to help keep you warm and an eye mask or flannel to help block out light. You begin by focusing on an intention or a purpose for your relaxation. This may be that you wish to relax, or it could be that there is something going on in your life that you want to gain inner guidance with. The key is to allow your body to set the intention, rather than your mind.

How to Take a Yoga Nidra Nap

- **Find somewhere comfortable to lie down** and relax (ideally not your bed). Cover yourself with a blanket and place an eye mask or flannel over your face to block out light and help you switch off.
- **Notice your thoughts** as they each come into your awareness. Instead of trying to prevent them from flowing, simply allow them to drift in and observe them as if you are watching clouds floating past in the sky, rather than engaging with them. Trust that you can come back to each of them later.
- **Turn your awareness to your breath** and take a full, deep breath, filling your lungs completely as your breathe in and exhaling any stale air with your out breath. Allow your breath to connect you with your body.
- **Sense into your body** and notice if there are any areas in particular drawing your attention. Stay with each of these areas and dialogue with them. Ask what intention your body would like you to hold for your yoga nidra nap. Listen for the sensation that you experience in reply.
- **Take a journey** around your body allowing each breath to connect you with suppressed feelings and emotions. Ask your body what it most wants you to know. Stay with the sensations you experience and rest for as long as you feel you wish. When you are ready to return from your rest take three deep breaths, rub your hands together, remove your eye mask, place your palms over your face and gently open your eyes, bringing your awareness back into the room.

To learn more about Yoga Nidra, visit the website where you can download a teleseminar recording during which I discuss the benefits of napping with Karen Brody.

The time is now for women to be BOLD and take the radical act of getting deep rest. Rest is healing, enlivens our life force, and connects us with the deep wisdom of our soul. When women lead from this place they are unstoppable.
Karen Brody

Be Happy for No Reason

While it is believed that some people are actually born with a higher 'happiness setpoint' than others, with 50% of our positivity being attributed to genes (Marci Shimoff, 2009) psychologists widely believe it's only 10% to do with our general circumstances (level of education, income, married/single) and 40% a learned skill, almost like knitting. This large, learned chunk can be changed quickly because it is to do with your day-to-day behaviour and how you think about yourself and others.

Top Tips to Boost Happiness

1. Spend more time with positive people – It is useful to notice how you feel when you are around the different people in your life and become aware of who the positive players are, as well as the negative ones. Surround yourself with as many positive people as possible and notice the impact they have on your own level of positivity and flexible thinking.

Positive people will help keep you motivated and uplifted on your journey through life. Negative people will shut down your dreams, take away your confidence and disempower you.

Keep away from people who belittle your ambitions. Small people always do that, but the really great make you feel that you, too, can become great.
Mark Twain

2. Talk to Oprah – Who are the three most positive people you can think of? They might include someone you have known personally, the author of a book or a personality on TV.

When I ask clients this question many people list Oprah in their top three. I suggest that they draw or cut out a picture of her and keep it somewhere easily accessible. Then, whenever they are deliberating over a situation, turning molehills into mountains or feeling a bit down, I suggest they pull out the picture of Oprah and ask, 'What advice do you have for me right now?' and write whatever response comes to them.

Give it a try with your favourite role model!

3. Look on the Bright Side

Being positive in a negative situation is not naïve. It's leadership.
Oprah Winfrey

With each thought that enters your head you have a choice whether to engage with it or not. You can also choose to change any of your negative thoughts to positive ones and purposefully decide to look on the bright side of life.

When you experience an event that makes you feel angry, take a deep breath and find something positive you can take from the experience. For example, did it help you become more skilled at communicating your emotions, teach you to trust your instincts more, give you more appreciation for aspects of your life, strengthen a relationship, help you forgive someone or help you grow stronger as a person? This technique can help lower stress levels, ease pain and assist you in moving on much happier about the situation.

If you would like to learn more about how to switch your thinking and change your actions so that you can get the very best from whatever life sends your way, check out *Flip It* by Michael Heppell for further inspiration.

4. Stop Complaining – Regularly complaining and criticising negatively impacts our health because dwelling on negative things creates stress. Many people have habits around this that they are completely unaware of. In the book *A Complaint Free World*, Will Bowen suggests challenging yourself to go 21 days without complaining. The challenge is brilliant for helping you break through old beliefs and boosting your health.

To give the 21-day challenge a try, pop a bracelet or wrist band on one of your wrists and every time you find yourself complaining, criticising or unfairly judging someone else, move the band from one wrist to the other. The majority of people find that they will need to move their band from wrist to wrist around 20 times per day initially. But, after just a few days, most people find that they can easily go four or five days without having to move the band once!

5. Pay a kindness forward – I was first introduced to the pay it forward concept by Carol Newland, Founder of Worklife Architect. Paying it forward basically means doing a good turn without wanting something in return. If and when someone asks how to repay a favour, you request that they then pay forward instead.

David Hamilton talks about this passionately. In his book *Why Kindness Is Good for You*, he says that research has shown people who perform random acts of kindness for other people are happier and more positive. Acts of kindness do not need to be grand in scale; even very minor acts, like letting someone jump a queue or donating money to charity can be enough to produce a significant gain in terms of increased happiness and positivity levels.

Dr Robert Emmons, a psychologist and Lab Director at the University of California, suggests that paying a kindness forward can be the ultimate form of expressing true gratitude. It can serve as a 'key link between receiving and giving' moving the 'recipient to share and increase the very good they have received'.[74]

In 1997 Dr Emmons conducted a series of studies with Michael McCullough, a psychologist at the University of Miami, that led them to discover scientific evidence that when people regularly express gratitude for things, people and places they are appreciative of in their lives, each day they end up happier, healthier and more optimistic about the future.

Schedule Renewal

Strategic Renewal – including… longer sleep hours, more time away from the office and longer, more frequent vacations – boosts productivity, job performance and, of course, health.
Tony Schwartz

Wellness brings well-being. Schedule wellness treats into your daily, weekly and monthly schedule until they become second nature to you. Having things planned for the first few weeks or months can help ensure they happen. Whether it is a super green smoothie for breakfast, a fifteen-minute walk at lunchtime, soaking in a bath at the end of the day, a weekly massage or weekend spa break, enjoy being good to yourself as a new way of being. You deserve it.

British tea brand Twinings have a fantastic campaign titled *Take 10*. The concept of the campaign is to encourage people to put aside a little time each day to reconnect with themselves. By taking ten minutes out from the busyness of our non-stop modern world, we can relax, refresh and recharge.

Little breaks are incredibly important; so too are bigger ones! Just as you may need to schedule short breaks into your working day in order to ensure they happen, it is also important to plan ahead and safeguard your holiday entitlement. Organise your holiday time well in advance and openly communicate your intended leave dates as early into the year as possible.

Alisa Thiry, CEO of ALT Creatives and Odette Hotel Group, schedules several well-being retreats throughout the year in order to prevent burnout:

> *I have found some wonderful European spa resorts offering holistic treatments, nutritious food, and luxurious surroundings. Every few months I like to visit them to help me rest, re-energise, and return home feeling reinvigorated.*

Yahoo! CEO Marissa Mayer is another shining example of someone who has not been shy to take her holiday allowance. Instead of feeling guilty about going away she schedules a brief vacation every four months and openly communicates it with her colleagues. She says her holidays help her pace herself. This also makes her a more effective leader, because in modeling what she believes in, she gives other people permission to step up and claim the same.

Stop Juggling, Start Single-Tasking

Multitasking is a myth. Several studies have proven that unless we are doing very routine things it is impossible for the human mind to fully focus on more than one thing at a time. Eyal Ophir, who led a research study[75] at Stanford University, found that 'humans don't really multitask, we switch'. His team discovered that even trying to do more than one thing may impair cognitive control.

Task switching takes longer than single-tasking because we need to refocus every time we switch back to our original task.

> *Out of all the things our mind does, that switching function is the most depleting.*
> Amishi Jha

Think about times when you have tried to write an e-mail when on the phone and ended up missing large parts of the conversation, or when you have been in a meeting and barely taken in any of the discussion because you have been trying to read through a report on another topic at the same time.

When multitasking, we often end up doing several things poorly rather than one thing really well. Little harm can come to us when we attempt multitasking at our desk or a meeting, but the consequences whilst driving, operating machinery or cooking can be more severe.

It is so easy, for example, to become distracted by something on the radio whilst driving and miss the turning that our GPS gave, or to cause an accident because we drove through a red light whilst on the phone. Even using a hands-free kit impairs our ability to focus on the road when at the wheel. It is much safer to save your phone calls for when you are stationary.

I have burned many meals and destroyed several saucepans as a result of trying to do too many things at once, whilst attempting to cook for myself and my family. Now that I have two children under the age of three I realise that I really need to concentrate when I am in the kitchen and turn things off if I need to leave the room for any reason; otherwise I would be putting our lives at risk of fire.

You can overcome your impulse to multitask by working out your most focused period of the day and turning that time into your power-hour(s).

Whether you are a morning person, work best after lunch or like to be a night owl, carve this time out to apply yourself fully to the most important project that you need to complete and cancel out anything that might distract you from it.

Do whatever it takes to protect this time of your day and plan all other things around it.

Try to set a specific time and time limits for checking email, voicemail, social media and other web-based information so that these things do not swallow up the time in between your power hours.

Prioritise Your Rocks

There is a popular time management metaphor that uses a glass jar, rocks, stones, pebbles, sand and water to demonstrate how to approach your daily priorities. The concept is that unless you place the rocks in the jar first, there will not be enough space to fit the stones, pebbles, sand or water.

The rocks represent the most important things in our lives – our health, family, friends, life goals, main projects and taking time out. When these things are prioritised first, there is always room to fit in the other 'stuff' – but if we allow our lives to be filled up by the less important things, we leave little or no time for what is truly important for us.

We can use this metaphor to help us plan out any time frame we want.

Many people beat themselves up towards the end of the year when they realise they have not accomplished the goals they set for themselves in January. Usually this is because they allowed lots of little things to take up their time and energy, rather than saving space for what truly mattered to them.

Stop doing anything that is not valuable.

Take back control of your time. You can afford to press pause in order to plan ahead. You can afford to press pause in order to rest and reflect. Your happiness and well-being depend on it.

Modern life bullies us to speed up our lives… but in racing against the clock, all we do is stress ourselves out. Going faster doesn't give us more time – it makes us feel that we're always behind. We battle against time, our imagined enemy.
Richard Koch

Imagine your year ahead as a glass jar; what are the key things that you would like to incorporate? Plan these in ahead of time and set reminders to yourself to check on your progress towards to make sure they happen.

In the same way, apply this process to your month, your week and your day ahead to help you focus on what is really important, and ensure you sustain the energy and momentum required to achieve your desired success.

Know When You Are Done

There is always something more that can be done on any project. Establishing a clear definition of what being 'done' looks like, identifying when you have reached that point, and then giving yourself permission to call it a day is crucial to preventing and overcoming burnout.

Many people I work with do not have a problem with organisation skills or fitting lots of things into a short space of time. In fact, they tend to be extremely good at these things up to a certain point. What they struggle with is knowing when to stop.

When I was a young university student studying Economics with modern foreign languages at the University of Surrey, I remember being taught the Law of Diminishing Returns. The example of fertiliser was used to explain how this law works. When a farmer uses fertiliser in crop production it improves the

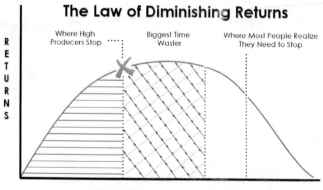

The Law of Diminishing Returns

RETURNS

Where High Producers Stop

Biggest Time Waster

Where Most People Realize They Need to Stop

INVESTMENT: Time, Energy, Money, Etc

amount of crops that he can yield; but at some point if the farmer continues to add fertiliser, the yield will not increase; moreover if the farmer adds further fertiliser the yield will begin to decrease.

This same principle can be applied to our working lives. Our productivity plateaus and then diminishes after a certain point.

When we go beyond this point our creativity and productivity rapidly diminish, and if we continue pushing ourselves to work more and more we start to burnout and head quickly downhill.

Work more; accomplish less.

If we allow ourselves to take time out and recuperate from the effects of operating at high and intense levels of productivity, we are able to maximise our overall long-term output levels because we stay connected to our creativity and are therefore more able to focus and achieve incredible outcomes whenever we reapply ourselves.

When you employ time-saving techniques in order to be more productive, ensure you set an 'end date' definition so that you stop when you are done. This may challenge you at first. Stay with it. You will soon begin to notice the great benefits this will bring.

In his book *You Can Have What You Want*, Michael Neill describes how 'being done' felt when he experienced it for the first time:

> *One day I had an extraordinary experience that I couldn't quite believe. It was around 4 p.m. and I looked into my book to see what was next. To my amazement, there wasn't anything left on my list. I was done with my work for the day... Of course, if I had wanted to, I could have found things to do – my projects hadn't all magically completed themselves. But I had done enough – I had done what I set out to do.*

Believe in Yourself

The vision you have developed for your future is likely to involve taking action towards experimenting with things that you have not done for a while or are completely new to. Burnout has a tendency to knock our confidence. It is important to practice believing in yourself.

It's so important to believe in yourself. Believe that you can do it, under any circumstances. Because if you believe you can, then you really will. That belief just keeps you searching for the answers, and then pretty soon you get it.
Wally Amos

I earlier explained the benefit of feeling your fear in order to move through it. Confidence often does not emerge from within us until we accept our fears and take action. From taking action our confidence kicks in. By taking further action, over and over, it grows and grows. We start seeing positive results from the actions we took, and our confidence is further strengthened.

Each time we take action our confidence grows and dispels our fear so that the next time we approach it, the fear is less and the confidence we feel is more. At the same time our competence continues increasing. The combination of confidence and competence makes our biggest dreams and seemingly impossible goals possible.

If I have the belief that I can do it, I will surely acquire the capacity to do it, even if I may not have it at the beginning.
Mahatma Gandhi

Whenever you notice your self-belief needs a boost, remind yourself of what you will gain by going for it, taking action and achieving the results you want to create. Notice how fulfilling it feels to visualise your dreams manifesting; imagine how much more fulfilling it will be when you actually start taking action and making them happen.

Give yourself permission to give things a go, for things not to have to be 100% perfect. Give yourself permission to do an ok job as well as an amazing job. Remind yourself that is ok to fail and that it will always ultimately be the learning you take from any experience that truly makes it worthwhile.

Ask for Help

If you have struggled in the past because of a tendency to put the needs of others before yourself, even when you are already running on empty, then it is likely that you find it equally difficult to ask for help. Many people I work with explain that while they find it easy to give unconditionally, they have a hard time receiving without feeling indebted to the other person. As a result, they keep giving without allowing anyone else to return the favour.

It is incredibly important to balance giving with receiving in order to prevent burnout. Help can come from those we are closest to like our friends, partners and family members as well as those we work with and even from strangers.

Asking is the beginning of receiving. Make sure you don't go to the ocean with a teaspoon. At least take a bucket so the kids won't laugh at you.
Jim Rohn

Take a huge metaphorical bucket and allow it to fill to the brim with help and support that will enable you to go for your dreams and manifest everything on your vision board. Allow the help to come to you and allow yourself to ask for help.

Obtaining consistent support is crucial to sustaining your success. As our society has started to move away from the close-knit communities we used to live in, many people, especially city dwellers, can find themselves with very little or no locally based support. Joining associations in your community or regional interest-based groups can be a wonderful way of expanding your support network, even if just for exploring new ideas and inspiration. Working with a coach is another great way to ensure you have someone by your side to be a cheerleader to your success.

Smart Steps to Ask for More Help

1. Start Small – Ask for help with something small that you would usually have struggled with on your own today. For example, ask your partner to wash up after your evening meal this evening, ask a strong-looking stranger on a bus to help you lift your case onto the luggage rack or pay for a taxi home from the station instead of pushing yourself to walk back in the pouring rain. Remember changing things, even the smallest things, is worth it. You are worth it. All the small things you ask for help with will combine to have a cumulative effect! And they will empower you to ask for even bigger help.

2. Shift from Surviving to Thriving – If you notice yourself resenting other people who seem to achieve things with grace and ease and find yourself getting caught up in the drama of your struggle (and those of others), take a step back, breathe and rescue yourself. Staying in the struggle only creates more struggle. When someone asks you 'How are things going?' and you respond 'Surviving!' – you are caught in your struggle. Step back from it and remind yourself that you are in charge of whether or not you struggle. You have a choice: Continue Surviving? Or Commit to Thriving!

3. Avoid Busy, Busy, Busy – When you're just about to ask for help and a little voice in your head says 'no one can do it better than me' or 'in the time it takes to explain this to someone else I could do it myself', take a deep breath and notice that you are stepping back into old patterns of doing too much. There are plenty people who can and will do things just as good as you.

The first time you explain things before handing over the reins it may feel like it will take you longer than it would to just do it yourself. Actually, it is a wisely spent time investment though because once you have shown them the ropes, they will not need you to explain it to them again.

It is also empowering to other people in your life when you trust them enough to step aside and allow them to do things for themselves. Start by releasing the jobs you hate. There are certain things in our lives that we all dread and keep putting off, so much so that they never get done. The beauty is that what one person hates doing, another person enjoys with passion! Release the jobs you hate by giving them to someone who can get them done for you. If it is the cleaning you hate, hire a cleaner; if you loathe ironing, have it done by someone else. Hire a gardener, an accountant, someone to run your errands – whomever you need for whatever you hate. You'll experience more energy just knowing all those jobs that used to niggle and drain you are getting done. Plus you are freeing up more time to do more of the things you love – increasing your overall happiness levels, which will have a positive impact on everyone around you.

4. Build Bigger – Once you have experienced success at letting go of struggling with some of the little things, challenge yourself to gradually ask for more and more help. Keep building on the amount of help you reach out for, little by little, step by step.

Look at what you have coming up in the next few days or weeks and find something that you are currently planning to organise or run all by yourself. It may be an evening dinner you have planned with friends, a presentation you are delivering at work or a task like clearing out your garage.

Break the event or project down into chunks and think of creative ways that you could ask for help with different elements of it. For example, ask your dinner guests to each bring a dish or accompaniment for the meal, hire a cleaner or your teenager to smarten up the house before your guests arrive so that you do not have to, or have your partner agree to help set and clear the table, serve the drinks, and do the washing up afterwards.

Accept compliments graciously; when someone says well done or that you look great, do not discount them. Reply 'thank you' – really reflect back that you have heard them.

Create a Sacred Space

Many cultures throughout history have devoted considerable resources to the creation of sacred spaces where people could go to nourish and nurture their body, mind and soul. Yet we seem all too frequently to be swapping sacred structures for skyscrapers and forgetting to leave sufficient space for pick-me-up pit stops in between.

We all need somewhere we can go to escape the rat race and soothe our souls. Having somewhere healing to head to whenever we want to take a break can also help entice those of us with workaholic tendencies to make time to disconnect from the outside world, turn off our phone and create an oasis within which to rest, reflect and recharge.

Since taking ballet classes as a young girl, Bonita Stewart, Vice President of Partner Business Solutions at Google, has been a lifelong lover of ballet. She says that the ballet studio has always been a sacred space for her to escape to: 'something about having the barre, the wooden floor, the pianist, the instructor, made me feel as though all else was outside'.

Is there somewhere you can go to and completely unplug?

Many of my clients have found that creating their own sacred space at home is an effective solution.

Setting aside your own sacred space can be as simple as finding a special chair or cushion to sit on, or you may wish to designate an entire area, room or corner of your garden as your sanctuary. Creating your own oasis of calm can help to strengthen your sense of inner peace and tranquility.

Remember how good it felt as a child when you engaged with your inherent den-building skills and created a secret shelter, a place to spend time undisturbed? You might want to upscale things from cardboard boxes and sticky tape but the principles are the same. Engage your imagination, clear out your clutter, and reclaim a space to call your own.

Simple Steps to Create a Sacred Space

1. Location, Location – First you need to figure out where you want your sanctuary to be. Notice where you naturally feel most relaxed in your home, garden or office space. Wander around your environment and search for a spot that you can make your own. It might be somewhere you already naturally feel drawn to, or you might discover a neglected area you feel inspired to clear out and transform into your own special hide away.

2. Clear Clutter – Clear out anything from your space that depletes your energy. Choose only to have items, colours, materials and music that feel uplifting and relaxing. Trust your intuition and allow it to guide you in selecting treasures to introduce into to your space. Indulge your senses with luxurious fabrics, sensual smelling candles, pretty potted plants, a gentle wind chime or water feature.

3. Balance the Elements – To ensure the optimum flow of energy in your special space, include an equal balance of items or aspects representing each of the nourishing and controlling elements.

4. Care for Your Space – Set an intention for your space to be your special sanctuary for replenishment and relaxation. Make a wish or prayer for your space to bring blessings and peace for all who enter it. Keep it clean and well maintained and allow fresh air to circulate through the space regularly – spend time in it, enjoy it, and it will nourish and nurture your soul in return.

Set Self-Care Reminders

If I knew I was going to live this long, I'd have taken better care of myself.
Mickey Mantle

Self-care is a necessity, not a luxury. It is a way of life that is dependent on you developing new daily habits that will profoundly challenge your old self-worth and identity beliefs. It will also impact the lives of those around you in incredible ways.

Changing your priorities so that you truly practice self-care is completely possible, but in order to support the new neurological pathways that you are creating in your brain to replace your old conditioning of stress and struggle, you may need to set some self-care reminders to help keep you on track.

Some suggestions:

- Create a series of self-care 'stickies' (using post-it notes or make your own using pieces of coloured card and some scotch tape) with words or pictures on them that will remind you to get enough rest, nourish your body, clear your clutter, say no, let go of excessive commitments, prioritise your health, exercise, take a nap, etc. Pop them up around your home or workspace.
- Buy a pack of self-care cards and laminate them to use as coasters that you change on a regular basis or pop them in a glass jar or basket and pull a message each day before you break for lunch. By seeing you glow, others will naturally be uplifted and inspired to take better care of themselves, too. You might even like to encourage them by

giving them the gift of a pack of self-care cards. I highly recommend Cheryl Richardson's cards, which are also available as a smart phone app.

Being kind to yourself is contagious. It spreads to everyone you meet.
Cheryl Richardson

- Buy a plant or keep a vase of flowers on your desk. Whenever you water your plant or change your flowers, consciously do something caring for yourself too. Studies show that plants can induce your relaxation response – an added bonus to having them around.

Stay Flexible

Stay committed to your decisions, but stay flexible in your approach.
Tony Robbins

Being open to alternative solutions and ways of doing things is key to overcoming and avoiding burnout. The very fact that you are reading this chapter means that you have already started to shift your mindset and consider to commit to a different way of life. Staying flexible in your thinking will enable you to continue moving past old patterns of perfectionism.

The tools, techniques and exercises we've explored together will help you to more easily reconcile external changes and calmly confront challenging situations with the ability to integrate internal conflicts and balance inconsistencies. I encourage you to refer back to them regularly to help you continue confronting the way you previously approached problems or made predictions and assumptions. In doing so, you prevent old scenarios from repeating themselves by consciously choosing how you want to create your life.

Whenever you notice yourself on autopilot, make a deliberate, mindful decision to stop, breathe and explore a new approach. Making a conscious effort to escape old patterns is often all that is required to stimulate creativity and come up with new solutions. Allow yourself to be more spontaneous, try new things and mix up your regular routines.

Flexibility helps us to better handle the ups and downs of life, to adapt to change, view things from different vantage points, take risks and reconcile our mistakes. By being more open and fluid in our thinking we become more comfortable with spontaneity, attract more opportunities and access greater creativity as a result.

Top 5 Tips to Increase Your Flexibility:

1. List Your Rules and Routines – Over the course of a week begin to notice your habitual thoughts, responses and behaviours. Make a note of them and play with the idea of mixing things up and approaching them in an alternative way.

2. Practice Doing Things Differently – Spend an additional week experimenting with small changes to your usual habits (e.g., get out on the opposite side of the bed, use a different shower gel, eat something unusual for breakfast or take a different route to work).

This exercise will help live your life with more flexibility and show you that you can do things differently. It will also help you to become more aware of experiencing each moment, rather than moving through your day-to-day activities on autopilot.

Notice any rigidness or resistance that you experience in response to this exercise. It is natural to feel uncomfortable, but stay with it! Use this technique any time you become aware of old burnout blocks reappearing in your life to help you break through them.

3. Hand Over Control – If you usually choose what movie to watch on Friday night, where to take the kids on Saturdays or what to have for Sunday lunch, let someone else make the decisions. Step back and allow them the space to do it their way, without jumping in to criticise or judge. Go with it, even if it is not exactly as you would have liked it to be.

Instead of looking for ways you would have done it better, try to find all of the positive learning you can take from the experience of releasing the reins. How might you be able to replicate this in the workplace or other areas of your life? Don't sweat the small stuff. Keep challenging yourself to gradually let perfectionism and old habits of overcommitting go; this will help you to allow more help into your life and prevent old patterns from re-emerging.

4. Practise Active Listening – You perhaps have heard the phrase, 'The opposite of talking isn't listening; it's waiting'. It can be all too easy to cut someone else off before they have finished speaking because we think we know what they are going to say, or doubt they would have a valuable solution to offer. When we do this regularly to others they eventually stop sharing their opinions. Start asking and acknowledging those you usually dismiss. Take a risk and try out some of their suggestions – you are likely to be pleasantly surprised by the outcome.

5. Stop Forcing – Whenever you notice yourself pushing or forcing a desired outcome, press pause and breathe. With each breath focus on bringing a sense of flow back to your body and your mind. Actively move your body by getting outside and going for a walk, taking a swim, dancing to music, drawing or painting. Permit yourself to take a break from the project or situation and do something completely unrelated. This will help to release rigid thinking and regain creativity and flexibility.

Flexible Work Policies

Flexible thinking is paramount in terms of finding new ways of working that challenge the current corporate culture of overwork. Flexibility needs to come from the top down in order to develop more flexible work policies that support sustainable work patterns. Many organisations have started to consider the issue of workplace flexibility in an attempt to help people balance the seemingly increasing demands of both work and family life.

Telecommuting, flexi-time, compressed workweeks, job sharing and reduced schedules are examples of some current policies being introduced and trialed by forward-thinking companies. Many organisations report the great benefits that such policies have started to bring, not just to the employees utilising them, but also to business, profitability and productivity.

Policies that permit telecommuting can significantly reduce costs. According to a review conducted by Global Workplace Analytics[76] of 500 telecommuting studies, allowing telework has reduced attrition, saving $10,000-$30,000 on average, per employee. Remote working also reduces unscheduled absences, which typically cost employers $1,800 per employee, per year. Real estate rental costs decrease on average by $10,000 per full-time teleworker and relocation costs can be completely eliminated.

Cost savings are not the only benefit realised in these efforts. Many companies are finding that client satisfaction often increases as a result of job-sharing arrangements in particular, where two people share the responsibility of what would previously have been an account or project managed by one person. Kirsty Faichen, a partner at Herbert Smith Freehills, one of the world's leading law firms, has a job-share arrangement with another senior partner, Mike Coonan. Kirsty enthusiastically reports that the arrangement is proving extremely successful, both personally and professionally, because her clients gain the advantage of utilising 'two brains' instead of one.

Flexible work policies require flexible thinking *and* need flexibility in their implementation in such a way that creates a shift in corporate culture. Kirsty credits much of the success of her flexible working arrangement on the open and honest communication channels it fosters, in addition to the mutual trust and respect it engenders between partners at her firm.

The outdated model of an exemplary employee being the first person to arrive at the office, last to leave, willing to work over weekends and forgoing vacations needs to be replaced by the person who adds the most value to the organisation via the originality, quality and results of their work, regardless of where or for how long their work is carried out.

Applying the Pareto Principle

The top 20 percent of people, natural forces, economic inputs, or any other causes we can measure typically lead to about 80 percent of results, outputs, or effects.
Richard Koch

While studying economics at university, I was introduced to the Pareto principle, named after Italian economist Vilfredo Pareto who noticed that 80% of the land in Italy was owned by 20% of the population and that 20% of the pea pods in his garden held 80% of the peas. Pareto was so intrigued by these findings that he surveyed other countries and found similar distribution ratios. This principle has since been applied to various aspects of business, in addition to optimisation efforts in computer science, criminology statistics and health care resources revealing the presence of the 80/20 principle.

It was not until I started my own business that I decided to experiment with the Pareto principle. As slave to 80-hour work weeks, the *more = more* illusion I had succumbed to in the corporate world, undoubtedly contributed to my experience of burnout. I was keen to see whether a *less = more* approach could really work, not only in my personal life but also professionally.

I discovered that the key to achieving more in less time and with less effort depended on my ability to:

1. Clarify my priorities.
2. Focus my attention on what mattered most to me.
3. Let go of anything that contributed to busyness but didn't add significant value to my business.
4. Delegate and outsource.
5. Acknowledge rest, relaxation and recuperation as being vital to my creativity and productivity.

The result? I accomplished more with greater energy and increased time available for all the other areas of my life.

Two years after applying this principle I became pregnant and challenged myself to further harness the power of less. I reduced the average weekly hours spent working on my business from 40 down to 30. Again, I achieved more.

Today, as the very proud and happy mother of a toddler and expecting my second child, I have once again reduced the amount of hours I spend working on my business, averaging around 20 hours per week yet continue to experience greater results than ever before.

I am sharing this because if it is possible for *me*, it is possible for *you*, too.

Being self-employed definitely makes it easier to be flexible with working hours. When you are your own boss you decide when to work and when to take time out. I schedule my working days, weeks and months to fit my clients and my family. This gives me the ability to balance my commitments and freedom to spend my time as I choose.

Significantly reducing the number of hours that I work has not negatively impacted on my productivity or profitability. I enjoy spending time working on my business. I am passionate about my work and find it nourishes me.

In my experience with clients, being passionate about what you do certainly makes a huge difference to how you feel about spending time 'at work.' Those who love what they do and do what they love generally seem happier to spend more hours working than those pursuing careers that are personally unfulfilling. I deeply encourage you to pursue your passions and find work that feels purposeful. I love helping people reignite their inner passions by discovering the work they were born to do and plan to write a future book on that topic.

Whether you are unemployed, self-employed or working for someone else, I encourage you to make time for the things you are truly passionate about. Your energy and enthusiasm for the hours you spend working will increase as a result, even if you are not doing the work that you feel destined for.

The aforementioned Global Workplace Analytics report about the advantages of telecommuting states that 14% of Americans have changed jobs in order to shorten their commute, almost half have said their commute is getting worse, and two-thirds would consider taking another job to reduce their travel time. In terms of time saving, teleworking can make a huge difference in achieving better work/life balance.

If you are looking to learn how to escape office overwork, consider whether teleworking or some of the other flexi-work policies highlighted above could help you to reduce stress, work less and beat burnout. If flexi-work policies are not already in place within your organisation or are met with resistance by senior management, get flexible and creative with your thinking in order to find a way to promote change within the culture your organisation.

There is nothing more difficult to take in hand, more perilous to conduct, or more uncertain in its success, than to take the lead in the introduction of a new order of things.
Niccolo Machiavelli, *The Prince* (1532)

Successful change requires trust. If you can prove to your boss that flexi-working will enable you to be equally, if not more productive, then not only is it possible to have her support you in a new way of working, but you can inspire others to follow your lead and become a catalyst for much-needed corporate change.

Consider the following preparatory steps before introducing the concept of telecommuting to your superior:

1. Explore what parts of your role could be done remotely.
2. Pre-empt any potential concerns that your boss might have so that you can creatively find ways to overcome them.
3. Experiment with taking your work out of the office environment to see whether you have the discipline to work alone.
4. Quantify your current productivity and document it as evidence to present to your boss.
5. Practise asking directly and with confidence for what you want before approaching your boss with a flexible work suggestion.

Once you feel certain that you can successfully prove your ability to work remotely, ask for a trial period to demonstrate the benefits that flexible working can help you bring to your organisation. This will help to warm your boss to the concept before requesting him to commit to it as a permanent arrangement.

Need-to-Know Summary
- In transforming your life from burnout to brilliance you are moving through a creative process of releasing the old to

recreate yourself anew and discover how to more authentically express your true self.

- Experimenting with art can help you discover more about yourself and how to stay aligned with your brilliance.
- Gratitude can also help to powerfully shift your view of burnout from that of a curse to a blessing.
- Identify your true priorities and re-inject energy and attention where you most want it to go.
- *The Purpose Statement* exercise featured in this chapter will help you to sharpen the vision you hold for yourself for the future and pull you closer towards becoming the person you truly want to be.
- Connecting with a clear future vision can truly help to keep you aligned with the brilliance you have within and prevent you from reverting to any of your old burnout habits or patterns.
- Future Life Progression (FLP) is a cutting-edge visualisation tool that can help you take a snapshot of your future to gain valuable life learning.
- The *Future Vision Expansion Meditation* featured in this chapter will introduce you to FLP and help you to uncover as much of your future vision as possible.
- The key to harnessing the power of your future vision expansion meditation experience is to regularly replay the feelings you gained when surrounded by the positive energy of your future life aligned with your inner brilliance.
- The process of creating a Vision Board can help you to capture and externalise your inner desires for the future.
- You can use your Vision Board to help you set inspired goals for the future and develop a strategy for sustaining your energy and actions towards your vision.
- Use the *Wellness Balance Chart* featured in this chapter to help you remember to balance action with inaction.

- Consider what help you might need, what more skills you might want to develop and what other things might you need to consider in order to help fuel your future success.
- Top Ten Strategies for Sustained Success:

    1. Get Enough Sleep
    2. Be Happy for No Reason
    3. Schedule Renewal
    4. Stop Juggling, Start Single Tasking
    5. Prioritise Your Rocks
    6. Know When You Are Done
    7. Believe in Yourself
    8. Ask for Help
    9. Create a Sacred Space
    10. Stay Flexible

- By committing to make continued positive change within yourself and your own life, you literally move beyond burnout and transform your entire way of being from burnout to brilliance.
- When you move beyond burnout, you act as a catalyst for change and harness energy that extends far beyond yourself.

Moving Beyond Burnout

I sincerely hope this book has helped you to identify, challenge and move beyond the internal drivers and external factors that previously contributed to your experience of exhaustion and overload. Through exploring and practising the exercises, tools and techniques I've presented, I trust you've been able to connect with a deeper understanding and awareness of yourself, in addition to finding your own sustainable strategies for future success.

Change will not come if we wait for some other person, or if we wait for some other time. We are the ones we've been waiting for. We are the change that we seek.
Barack Obama

By committing to make continued positive change within yourself and your own life, you literally move beyond burnout and transform your entire way of being from burnout to brilliance.

Allow this transformation to be the beginning of a new chapter in your life. There will certainly be further opportunity for self-learning, growth and development, no matter your age or where you find yourself along life's path. Use the tools and techniques to help you continue moving forward with a calm confidence that you can stay present to the process and move beyond future challenges by staying connected to the things in life that truly matter the most to you with the steadfast commitment to creating a life you love.

Your new approach and attitude towards life will inevitably inspire others, although you may receive resistance at first from those around you who would prefer that you stayed the same; this is because the moment you start prioritising self-care, being more authentic and shining more brightly, you challenge them to do this for themselves also, which they may or may not be ready for. Be patient with others and keep leading by example.

Although the world is full of suffering, it is also full of the overcoming of it.
Helen Keller

As we uphold and take pride in our individual responsibility for being the change that we wish to see around us, we start to shift collective consciousness. The ramifications of our own change may initially only be felt by our families, friends and colleagues. However, I believe that with time, more and more people will be inspired to move away from fear, competition, and outdated command and control mindset to one that promotes peace, equality, collaboration and care for ourselves, each other and the protection of our planet.

When you move beyond burnout, you act as a catalyst for change and harness energy that extends far beyond yourself.

Perhaps one day, this shared consciousness will help foster the global solutions required to bring about the vast changes that our public and private organisations, governments and worldwide communities are so desperately calling out for.

Table 3.1: Wellness Balance Chart Example

Date	Energy	Deposit Transaction	Withdrawal	Wellness Balance
10th Oct	8 hours sleep and started day with energizing ritual, nutritious breakfast and 10 minutes of yoga.	300		300
10th Oct	Wrote tender for new business.		100	200
10th Oct	Outsourced one of my projects.	100		300
10th Oct	Took a 20 minute walk outside after lunch.	100		400
10th Oct	Led senior management team meeting.		300	100
10th Oct	Dealt with office relocation disagreement.		300	-200
10th Oct	Left work on time and listened to relaxation music during commute home.	100		-100
10th Oct	Went swimming, had dinner with a friend and got to bed at 10pm.	300		200

Table 3.2: Wellness Balance Chart

Date	Energy Transaction	Deposit	Withdrawal	Wellness Balance

Appendix 1

Children Live What They Learn, Dorothy Law Nolte

If children live with criticism, they learn to condemn.

If children live with hostility, they learn to fight.

If children live with fear, they learn to be apprehensive.

If children live with pity, they learn to feel sorry for themselves.

If children live with ridicule, they learn to feel shy.

If children live with jealousy, they learn to feel envy.

If children live with shame, they learn to feel guilty.

If children live with encouragement, they learn confidence.

If children live with tolerance, they learn patience.

If children live with praise, they learn appreciation.

If children live with acceptance, they learn to love.

If children live with approval, they learn to like themselves.

If children live with recognition, they learn it is good to have a goal.

If children live with sharing, they learn generosity.

If children live with honesty, they learn truthfulness.

If children live with fairness, they learn justice.

If children live with kindness and consideration, they learn respect.

If children live with security, they learn to have faith in themselves and in those about them.

If children live with friendliness, they learn the world is a nice place in which to live.

Appendix 2

The Self as Organising Principle of Physis

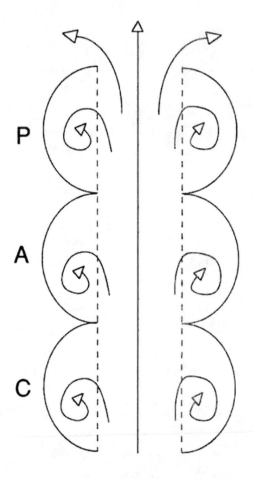

Source: Clarkson, P. (1992) Transactional Analysis
Psychotherapy: An Integrated Approach, London: Routledge.

Appendix 3

7 Key Chakras

Endnotes

Foreword

1 Conducted by Wonderful Pistachios, February 2013.

2 According to the American Cancer Society who researched the health of 123,000 people over the course of fourteen years.

3 Study conducted by Finnish Institute of Occupational Health, September 2012.

4 Conducted by OnePoll on behalf of Good Technology.

5 According to the Government's Health and Safety Executive.

6 According to a study conducted by the European Foundation for the Improvement of Living and Working Conditions for the period 2011-2012.

7 According to a study in 2009 by Buffalo University researchers testing the memory of rats.

8 *Effects of the 2011 Duty Hour Reforms on Interns and Their Patients*, JAMA Intern Med, 2013; 173(8):657-662

9 According to a 2012 report published by the official newspaper of the Communist Youth League, the *China Youth Daily*.

10 According to Trade Union Congress analysis of official figures published for 2011.

11 A study published in the Journal of Psychosomatic Research in 2010 found that burnout can be a predictor of mortality in a ten-year prospective register linkage study. http://www.management.tau.ac.il/Eng/_Uploads/dbsAttachedFiles/RP_1 57_Shirom.pdf

12 In an article published by the *Daily Mail* on 20th August 2013: http://www.dailymail.co.uk/news/article-2398415/Mor itz-Erhardt-dies-High-flying-bank-intern-died-working-crazy-hours-written-huge-pressure-succeed.html

Introduction

13 In the USA workplace stress costs more than $300 billion each year in health care, missed work and stress reduction according to American Institute of Stress, NY.

Part 1: Discovery

14 Jenny's name has been changed to protect her identity.

15 A vision board is a collage of images and phrases that inspire you to stay aligned with your true self and take positive action towards your future. See the chapter in the third part of this book, titled *Creating a Vision to Inspire You*, for full details on how to create a powerful vision board to optimise your health, wealth, relationships and wellbeing.

16 According to statistics issued by the NHS Information Centre, UK.

17 Quoted in *Time* article 'Can We Become Addicted to Stress?' by Katherine Schreiber, 6th September 2012: http://health land.time.com/2012/09/06/can-we-become-addicted-to-stress/

18 Pick, M (2011) Are You Tired and Wired? USA: Hay House Inc., 15.

19 Simpson, KR (2011), Overcoming Adrenal Fatigue, Canada: New Harbinger Publications, Inc.

20 According to the Great British Sleep Survey http://www.greatbritishsleepsurvey.com/2012report/

21 Published by AVG Technologies, May 2013

22 Conducted in July 2013 by Vouchercodespro.co.uk – featured in *Huffington Post* article *More than 60 Percent of British Women Check Their Phones During Sex*, 24th July 2013 by Dominque Mosbergen: http://www.huffingtonpost.com/2013/07/24/phones-during-sex-british-survey_n_3640820.html?1374680411 &ncid=edlinkusaolp00000008

23 Stewart, I. and Joines, V. (1987) *TA Today: A New Introduction to Transactional Analysis*, Chapel Hill: Lifespace Pub.

24 See Appendix 1

25 Based on Twelve Injunctions model presented by Stewart, I. and Joines, V. (1987) *TA Today: A New Introduction to Transactional Analysis*, Chapel Hill: Lifespace Pub.

26 'Breaking the Box' in *Passionate Supervision*, Robin Shohet, ed., Jessica Kingsley Publishers (2007)

Part 2: Recovery

27 Law, Sung Ping (1986). "The Regulation of Menstrual Cycle and Its Relationship to the Moon". *Acta Obstetricia et Gynecologica Scandinavica* **65** (1): 45–8

28 Research published in *Effects of insufficient sleep on circadian rhythmicity and expression amplitude of the human blood transcriptome*, edited by Joseph S Takahashi, Howard Hughes Medical Institute, University of Texas Southwestern Medical Center, Dallas, Texas, 23rd January 2013. http://www.pnas.org/content/early/2013/02/20/1217154110

29 Safety precaution: if you do not have a fireplace where you can safely burn your paper, please find another safe method to do so, or alternatively bury your paper in the ground with the intention of releasing your beliefs.

30 Presented by Sue O'Brien, CEO of Norman Broadbent at the Womensphere Europe Summit 2013: Creating the Future – Europe and the World

31 http://www.masaru-emoto.net/english/water-crystal.html

32 See Appendix 2

33 See Appendix 3

34 Clarkson (1992) describes the ego-states in the individual self being energized by inner core energy and provides a diagram indicating, with an arrow to represent aspiration, the upward direction of Physis as it transcends Child, Adult, and Parent ego-states. See Appendix 2.

35 Reid, H., Fordham, M., & Adler, G. (Eds.) (1954, p. 371). *The collected works of C. G. Jung: The symbolic life*. Princeton, NJ:

Princeton University Press.

36 Sigmund Freud, Case Histories II (PFL 9) p. 132

37 *The Biology of Belief,* Bruce Lipton, 2005, Cygnus Books. David Hamilton, It's the Thought That Counts, 2005, David Hamilton.

38 Robinson, Lynn. *Trusting Your Inner Voice in Times of Crisis,* Conneticut: GPP Life, 2009.

39 Robinson, Lynn. *Trust Your Gut: How the Power of Intuition Can Grow Your Business,* New York: Kaplan Business, 2006.

40 High vibrational food means food that has not been chemically treated, does not contain artificial additives or preservatives, and has been organically grown or reared and slaughtered with respect.

41 E. Z. Zimmer, W.P. Fifer, Y-I. Kim, H. R. Rey, C. R. Chao and M.M. Myers, 'Response of the premature fetus to stimulation by speech sounds', Early Human Development, 1993, 33(3), 207-15.

42 Report issued by Office for National Statistics, 31st March 2011, *Mothers in the Labour Market* http://www.ons.gov.uk/ons/dcp171776_234036.pdf

43 Melissa A. Milkie, Sarah B.Raley, and Suzanne M. Bianchi, "Taking on the Second Shift: Time Allocations and Time Pressures of US Parents with Preschoolers", Social Forces 88, no 2 (2009): 487-517

44 Deborah Lader, Sandra Short, and Jonathan Gershunny, The Time Use Survey, 2005: How We Spend Our Time: Amendment, 'Table 3.5: Time Spent on Housework and Childcare as Main and Secondary Activities with Rates of Participation by Sex, 2000 and 2005', Office for National Statistics, Crown, 2006.

45 Scott S. Hall and Shelley M. MacDermid, *"A Typology of Dual Earner Marriages Based on Work and Family Arrangements",* Journal of Family and Economic Issues 30, no 3 (2009):220.

46 Women Matter: Making the Breakthrough, McKinsey 2012

47 Women on Boards, Gov.uk report, February 2011 https://www.gov.uk/government/uploads/system/uploads/at tachment_data/file/31480/11-745-women-on-boards.pdf

48 Women Matter 1012: Making the Breakthrough, McKinsey & Company

49 Government Equalities Office, conducted by Ipsos MORi, sample of 1,071 adults in Great Britain aged 16+. 20-24 February 2010, published 11 March 2010. (59% of those surveyed believe that single-sex senior management teams were more likely to think the same way and so make poor decisions and 61% believed that businesses are losing out on talent by having fewer women in senior roles).

50 Do Men and Women Lead Differently? Who's Better? 23rd March 2010, Ronald E Riggio, Cutting Edge Leadership: http://www.psychologytoday.com/blog/cutting-edge-leadership/201003/do-men-and-women-lead-differently-whos-better

51 Women Take Care, Men Take Charge: Stereotyping of US Business Leaders Exposed, 19th October 2005, Catalyst Study, Knowledge Center: http://www.catalyst.org/know ledge/women-take-care-men-take-charge-stereotyping-us-business-leaders-exposed

52 Superwoman Syndrome is the term being used to describe women who struggle to 'be all things to all people'. Linda Ellis Eastman, ed., Overcoming the Superwoman Syndrome (Prospect, KY: Professional Woman Publishing, 2007).

53 You can download the podcast recording of our conversation from the website for this book: www.jaynemorris.com

54 http://www.aspirewomen.co.uk

55 Name changed to protect identity.

56 Speier, Cheri; Valacich, Joseph. Vessey, Iris (1999). "The Influence of Task Interruption on Individual Decision Making: An Information Overload Perspective". *Decision Sciences* 30.

57 http://www.csun.edu/science/health/docs/tv&health.html

58 Sarah Perez, Techcrunch, 2nd July, 2012, http://tech crunch.com/2013/07/02/80-of-americans-work-after-hours-equaling-an-extra-day-of-work-per-week/.

59 http://www.tvlicensing.co.uk/resources/library/BBC/ME DIA_CENTRE/TeleScope_report.pdf

60 http://www1.good.com/news/press-releases/current-press-releases/161098825.html

61 http://chrissybshow.tv/index.php/portfolio-view/declutter-your-life/

62 http://stakeholders.ofcom.org.uk/market-data-research /market-data/communications-market-reports/cmr11/

63 *News is bad for you – and giving up reading it will make you happier*, Rolf Dobelli, *The Guardian*, Friday 12th April 2013.

Part 3: Brilliance

64 http://www.bbc.co.uk/worldservice/specials/144_powerof-music/

65 www.annejirsch.com

66 'Developing Effective Pre-performance Routines in Golf', Journal of Applied Sport Psychology, Volume 22, Issue 1, 2010, Stewart T Cotterill, Ross Sanders, Dave Collins.

67 Luthans F., & Youssef, C.M. (2004). Human, social, and now positive psychological capital management: Investing in people for competitive advantage, Organizational Dynamics, 33(2), 143-160

68 'Psychological Capital and Employee Performance: A Latent Growth Modeling Approach', Suzanne J Peterson, Fred Luthans, Bruce J Avolio, Fred O Walumbwa, Zhen Zhang, *Personnel Psychology*, Vol 64, Issue 2, 427-450, Summer 2011.

69 Referenced by Bronwyn Fryer, 'Sleep Deficit: The Performance Killer' *Harvard Business Review* 84, no 10 (2006): 53-59, http://hbr.org/2006/10/sleep-deficit-the-performance-killer

70 Dhand, Rajiv; Sohal, Harjyot (2007). 'Good sleep, bad sleep! The role of daytime naps in healthy adults'. *Current Opinion in Internal Medicine* **6**: 91. doi:10.1097/01.mcp.000024 53.92311.d0

71 Lahl, Olaf; Wispel, Christiane; Willigens, Bernadette; Pietrowsky, Reinhard (2008). 'An ultra short episode of sleep is sufficient to promote declarative memory performance'. *Journal of Sleep Research* **17** (1): 3–10. doi:10.1111/j.1365-2869.2008.00622.x

72 Dr Mednick, Sara (2007) Take a Nap: Change Your Life, Workman Publishing. New York

73 McEvoy, RD; Lack, LL (2006). 'Medical staff working the night shift: Can naps help?'. *The Medical journal of Australia* **185** (7): 349–50.

74 Emmons, Robert (2013) *Gratitude Works! A 21-Day Program For Creating Emotional Prosperity*, Jossey-Bass, California USA

75 Ophir, Eyal; Nass, Clifford; Wagner, Anthony (2009) Cognitive Control in Media Multitaskers, PNAS 2009 106 (37) 15515-15517; doi: 10.1073/iti0937106

76 http://www.globalworkplaceanalytics.com/resources/costs-benefits

CHANGE
MAKERS
BOOKS

Changemakers publishes books for individuals committed to
transforming their lives and transforming the world. Our
readers seek to become positive, powerful agents of change.
Changemakers books inform, inspire, and provide practical
wisdom and skills to empower us to create the next chapter of
humanity's future.
Please visit our website at www.changemakers-books.com